NEVER TOO LATE

13 INSPIRING REAL-LIFE STORIES
BY
13 DEBUT AUTHORS

AF651787

COMPILED BY

DR. PRAVEEN SRINIVASAN

AUTHOR OF FICTIONAL NOVEL "7"

Clever Fox® PUBLISHING

Chennai • Bangalore

CLEVER FOX PUBLISHING
Chennai, India

Published by CLEVER FOX PUBLISHING 2025
Copyright © Dr. Praveen Srinivasan 2025
Cover Design by: Natesan Mohhan

All Rights Reserved.
ISBN: 978-93-6707-866-2

This book has been published with all reasonable efforts taken to make the material error-free after the consent of the author. No part of this book shall be used, reproduced in any manner whatsoever without written permission from the author, except in the case of brief quotations embodied in critical articles and reviews.

The Author of this book is solely responsible and liable for its content including but not limited to the views, representations, descriptions, statements, information, opinions and references ["Content"]. The Content of this book shall not constitute or be construed or deemed to reflect the opinion or expression of the Publisher or Editor. Neither the Publisher nor Editor endorse or approve the Content of this book or guarantee the reliability, accuracy or completeness of the Content published herein and do not make any representations or warranties of any kind, express or implied, including but not limited to the implied warranties of merchantability, fitness for a particular purpose. The Publisher and Editor shall not be liable whatsoever for any errors, omissions, whether such errors or omissions result from negligence, accident, or any other cause or claims for loss or damages of any kind, including without limitation, indirect or consequential loss or damage arising out of use, inability to use, or about the reliability, accuracy or sufficiency of the information contained in this book.

ACKNOWLEDGMENTS

This book, my first as a compiler, would not have been possible without the support and encouragement of so many people. To them, I owe my deepest gratitude.

First and foremost, I thank my parents, Mr. C.P. Srinivasan and Mrs. S. Sasikala, for their unwavering belief in me and my dreams.

My heartfelt thanks go to my dearest brother, Naveen Srinivasan, for appreciating every piece I've ever written and shared—and always asking for more.

To my teachers and mentors—thank you for your guidance, inspiration, and invaluable feedback. Your wisdom helped me refine my work and recognize its strengths.

I am eternally grateful to God for being my constant through every high and low, guiding me at every step.

To my wonderful friends, scattered across the globe—thank you for your unwavering support, honest advice, diverse perspectives, and for walking alongside me on this journey called life.

A special thanks to Clever Fox Publishing for believing in this unique compilation—13 real-life stories by 13 debut authors—and for providing a platform to share these voices with the world.

I extend my deepest gratitude to Mr. Natesan Mohhan, whose exceptional talent and dedication brought the cover of 'Never Too Late' to life. As his debut design project, his creativity has set the perfect visual tone for this book. Thank you for turning my vision into art.

Lastly, and most importantly, I thank you, my readers. This book was born from a conversation with friends who shared their desire to write but didn't know where or how to begin. Inspired, I reached out to many aspiring writers, encouraging them to share their real-life stories. Today, I am proud to introduce 13 debut authors to the world—may this be the first of many books from their pens.

If you wish to attempt something, leave fear behind and take that first step forward.

Thank you all, from the bottom of my heart.

Always Yours
Dr. Praveen Srinivasan
Author of fictional novel "7"

ABOUT THE COMPILER OF NEVER TOO LATE

Dr. Praveen Srinivasan, Ph.D., Chartered MCIPD

Author of fictional novel "7"

Dr. Praveen Srinivasan is a seasoned HR and administration professional with over 14+ years of experience, specializing in strategic talent management, employee relations, succession planning, competency mapping, change management, Performance Management and organizational development. Currently serving as the **Head of Human Resources and Administration at a private company in Dubai, UAE**, he excels in aligning HR initiatives with business objectives, driving employee engagement, and fostering a culture of continuous learning.

Key Highlights:

- **Expertise:** Strategic HR planning, talent acquisition, performance management, employee engagement, and compliance with labour laws.
- **Leadership:** Proven ability to lead HR projects, manage cross-functional teams, and implement data-driven HR strategies.
- **Certifications:** Chartered Member of CIPD (Level 7), Certified Performance & Competence Developer (CPCD).
- **Publications & Research:** Authored papers on competency mapping with a focus on bridging skill gaps in manufacturing industries.
    - Written a fictional story book titled "7" published by Clever Fox Publishers which is available in all leading online platforms.
- **Awards:** Recognized as a **Best HR Practice Leader** for outstanding contributions.
- **Multilingual:** Fluent in English and Tamil, with working knowledge of Hindi and Telugu.
- **Guest Lectures:** Given on various topics at various institutes not limited to "Competency Based Interviewing Skills", "Time Management", "Goal Setting", "Campus to Corporate", "Value addition & Certification courses for HR", "Where Are You Now", "Placement Grooming", "Competency Mapping", "Individual Development Plan", "Career

Progression Vs. Stability", "Usefulness of Final Year Project", "Brand Yourselves", "Workload Vs Expectation Vs Salary"

Education:

- Advanced Diploma in Strategic People Management (CIPD Level 7) - UK
- Ph.D. in Management (India)
- MBA in HR & Marketing (India)
- BE in Mechanical Engineering (India)

A dynamic leader, Dr. Praveen Srinivasan combines academic rigor with practical HR solutions to enhance organizational performance and employee satisfaction.

LinkedIn:

Contact Details: cpspraveen@gmail.com
Instagram ID: cpspraveen

CONTENTS

22-YEAR-OLD BOY

SRIHARAN

This entire chapter was written by a 22-year-old boy. It explores the battling voices within not just me, but within each of us. These voices shape who we were, who we are and who we'll become. There lies something in those voices that is far beyond what we know, and they make us aware whether we have done things right or wrong.

Every single one of us hears a voice speaking to us all the time. People often say that the voice comes from the heart, and they also claim that our heart doesn't lie. However, there is a problem: not everything we hear comes from the heart. It is a constant battle within our thoughts, but the crazy part is that we don't even know which one wins the battle. In the end, we tend to believe our thoughts even if they don't come from the heart. As time passes, we subconsciously lean toward believing in our inner voice, which may not even come from the heart. It's like having a toxic friend with you all the time. Now, let me explain it to you with a short story.

Most of you might have seen this movie "The Lion King " which was released in 1994. For those who didn't know the movie yet, this movie is an animated movie of a forest where a lion is the king of the jungle, and the name of the lion is Mufasa. He is brave, strong, responsible, and most importantly, he loves his forest and serves as the protector of the jungle. But Mufasa has a brother named "Scar", an ambitious, cunning, manipulative and jealous lion who wants the throne and is ready to do whatever he is capable of to claim the throne. Also, Mufasa had a naughty little boy named "Simba" who was the next heir to the throne. Scar killed his brother with a cunning plan and made Simba and others believe that Simba was the one who killed Mufasa, and Scar declared himself the king of the jungle. Simba ran far away carrying the guilt that he killed his father, and the rest of the story is Simba coming back to save the jungle and to avenge his father's death. If you haven't watched it yet, just go watch it. I assure you, it's worth your attention.

The point of my thoughts about this movie is that, similar to the story, each of us has two lions inside of us, each representing different personalities. One is "Mufasa" and the other is "Scar". When Mufasa rules the jungle, it is filled with greenery, freshwater and happiness. In contrast, under Scar's rule, the forest falls into darkness, leading to collapse.

It's up to each of us to nurture the right lion within. The more we listen to Mufasa- the voice that comes from our heart- the more it enriches and strengthens. The opposite happens when we start listening to what Scar tells us. But, as I said before, it's very hard to differentiate these voices; both of these voices feel the same until we learn to find the difference. Why am I telling all of this? Most of my life, I had no clue which voice I was hearing. Even now, it takes a lot of rethinking to find the right voice within me, but I'm confident that I'm on the right path in making myself a complete "Mufasa". I also believe that the pain we suffer makes our "Mufasa" stronger. So, here are three chapters of my life which made me aware of the voices within me.

Chapter 1: First love

Your first love is always a special one. I had my first love when I was 19, and it was a woman, but she was not a human; she was a lovely cat, and her name was Kemo. I don't mind calling a cat a woman because it doesn't matter when you look at something with such love. It wasn't love at first sight. She was a beautiful cat with golden hair, along with white strips flowing like rivers across those soft and fluffy golden locks. When she was brought to our house, she was just a regular cat to me; I wasn't even attached to her. Ten days passed, and I was in my grandma's house. I got a call from my mom, and she said that Kemo had been bitten by another cat the night before and was about to die. To be honest, I didn't feel much about it at that time. A few hours, I returned home, and when I saw her lying on the floor, my heart began to worry. She wasn't even able to move. She had a deep scratch across her belly and a severe bite mark on her neck; her golden, fluffy hair was matted with blood, and my mom had applied turmeric to the wounds. Kemo let out a low-pitch Meow; she couldn't meow loudly. I had never seen a cat cry before, and I didn't know how a cat cried. There were no tears in her eyes, but the sound she made felt like a cry of pain to me. Seeing that, I sat near her on the floor and rubbed her forehead to comfort her. Within a few seconds, she managed to wake up, though she was unsteady on her feet. Despite her condition, she stumbled toward me and put her claws on my thighs, trying to climb up. I pushed her back to help her. After climbing up, she lay on my thighs, silent. Every ten seconds or so, she would look at me and let out a small "Meow", and that was the moment I fell in love with her. Sitting there on the floor with Kemo on my thighs, I decided to take care of her and not let her die. Then, I sat there for a while, rubbing her forehead.

Days passed, and she started getting better and better every single day. My attachment to her grew deeper and deeper as time went on. From that day on, she would lie on my lap, and as I rubbed her forehead, she would lick my hands to do me a favour in return. She would always disturb me whenever I was at home, and apart from all of those cherishing moments with her, I was afraid. But why? I was afraid of losing her; the more I got attached to her, my fear of losing her grew. You remember the cat I told you about, a cat that bit Kemo on the neck and scratched her on the belly? It was still visiting our house, so I made sure to lock all the windows at night. I was confident that if Kemo grows stronger, she would be able to fight that cat back, but until then, I needed to protect her from that cat and the dogs in our street. Occasionally, Kemo would run out of our house. She eventually learned how to come back, but until she returned, my heart would race.

Three months passed, and one Sunday morning, Kemo ran out as usual. Eventually, she came back, but she had a slight red mark on her front right paw. It was noticeable only if you looked closely at her paws. I thought that she had gotten her paw on some kind of spike or something. I was doing some other work, but after almost an hour, she started to feel cranky. I thought she might have eaten something that made her feel that way. As time passed, she became weaker and weaker. Then I realised it was the mark on her paw. I thought of taking her to the hospital, but since it was Sunday, there were no veterinary hospitals.

So, we took her to a veterinary doctor's house. He wasn't there at first, so we had to wait for half an hour. When he finally arrived, I explained to him about the mark on her paws, and he gave her some kind of injection. I hoped once again that she would get better soon so we could play together like we had in those previous days. Within a few minutes, Kemo started to move less and less, and at some point, she wasn't moving. Her eyes were open, and the colour of her eyes changed to a slightly transparent colour. Her soul left her body as she was in my arms. For a few seconds, I couldn't believe that she was dead. Then, after a few seconds, my heart felt so heavy that I couldn't even cry. I took her to our grandma's house, which was nearby. When I carried her, I couldn't feel her; her skin felt loose, and she felt heavier than I was used to when I carried her. I took her to my grandma's backyard and buried her, then came back to my house. Even until that evening, my heart felt heavy, and I couldn't even cry. Then, at night, I had my first tear of losing her. I cried for a while, and even the next day, I couldn't handle the pain of losing her. To distract myself, I started watching a comedy reality show. Whenever my sight was out of the TV, my heart felt heavy. So, I binge-watched the show for the entire day for the next ten days. These were times when I felt like Kemo was still alive, but when I realised that she was not with me anymore, it would poke at my heart for a while. When I feel some pain, without a second thought, I would distract myself from the situation. After a few days, I started to feel better, and those memories faded gradually. But now I realise that I shouldn't have ignored the feeling of losing her. Those distractions made me not think about the tragedy, but they didn't make me feel better. They distracted me, but they did not make me strong; distracting myself made me even weaker and afraid of my voice. The scar within me gave me temporary satisfaction and never let me listen to what Mufasa told me. My Mufasa grew weaker as I stopped listening to it, even though I didn't feel the pain after a few days. I was emotionally weaker than I was before; my interest in other things diminished.

Instead of naming this chapter "First love", I should have named it "First heartbreak", but I'm saving it for something that occurred later. I think that would be suitable for a real heartbreak situation. Even though I wasn't listening to my Mufasa, I had something that made my Mufasa strong, which is what contributed to my emotional strength in the long run: getting myself physically fit. The next entire chapter is about that. Now, let's just call it the end of the chapter and jump to the next one.

Chapter 2: The Outer Self

Growing up, I was a chubby boy, but somehow, with somehow, with a random strike on my head, I started to exercise. I wasn't doing it right, but I was doing something, and it felt right to me. Days passed, and I was getting lean; I continued to learn different ways to exercise, and I was becoming fit as days went by. All those days, I knew nothing about nutrition or fitness; all I wanted to do was to stay lean and continue my daily exercise routine.

After two years of exercising, one day when I was taking a bath, I felt my muscles were too loose, and even though I was doing my exercise for almost two years, I hadn't made any significant progress other than getting lean. I was lean, but I wasn't strong enough. Standing there with the shower on, a voice stuck in my head encouraged me to go to the gym. The next evening, I went to a gym near my house and got a membership. The following day, I set up an alarm at 5 AM, woke up, drank a litre of water, brushed my teeth, put my shoes on and made my way to the gym, which was 3 kilometres away, on my cycle. As I continued to go to the gym over the next few months, my muscles started to gain strength. I met new people who were familiar with nutrition and fitness; they taught me that our body needs rest for at least one day a week for proper muscle recovery. I started eating healthy. When I say healthy, most might think of a strict diet plan, but it's not that; I just avoided the unhealthy items like high-oil foods, high sugar foods and processed foods. I also began to add more protein to my food. In the beginning, my whole day felt tiring, but as days passed, I started to feel more energetic. I was a student and wasn't earning back then, so I couldn't afford high-protein foods. Even when I buy chicken or lentils, I can't make them myself. I had to eat what my mom used to make. That's why I found an alternative to this problem: eating 3 whole eggs a day to somewhat compensate for my protein requirements. Even to this date, while I'm writing this, I eat 3 eggs a day and drink 1 litre of water right after waking up. I was not just going to the gym, I was also learning about food and health. I continued to go to the gym for the next two years. Well, I wasn't able to go to the gym daily, because I wasn't able to stay in a single place. I had to go to different places. And I couldn't afford to go to the gym, wherever I go, also going to the gym requires you to put in at least 2 hours of your day. It includes the travel time to the gym and preparing yourself to go to the gym. At times, staying fit kind of felt like a burden. Not just that, wherever you stay for longer, you'll have to find a gym there. And if there is no gym in the place that I go, it creates a sense of guilt for not working out. Not just that, right now when I am young, I could go to the gym and lift weights, but as I get older, I can't lift weights as I could right now. Also, lifting heavier weights for a very long time degrades your joints. With, all this, I don't mean to say that going to gym is bad, it the most awesome thing to do, but it depends on our priorities, if my priorities were to have up larger muscles or be a competing bodybuilder, it's the best option for me to continue going to gym for the rest of my life. But my priorities were simple: stay fit, stay strong, stay healthy and be active, all this both physically and mentally till the last breath. Also, I want to do it efficiently, I should be able to keep myself fit without going to the gym. That is when one day I decided to stop going to the gym, something I have been doing for the past 3 years. Then, with all that I have learned about my own body, for the past 3 years, I framed a workout plan for myself, which consists of working out for half an hour a day in the morning. At first, I doubted it, I thought it wouldn't work for me. But it's been more than a year since I made that decision, and I feel stronger and more active than I was when I went to the gym. These days, I sleep more than 7 hours a day, drink 1 litre of water right after waking up, do half an hour of exercise in the morning and eat 3 eggs a day along with some other nutritious food. Doing all this, I eat some unhealthy foods once in a while and skip some days of workout when I don't feel like working out, but it doesn't make me feel bad about myself and staying fit doesn't feel like a burden anymore. If there is something that I have learnt from this experience, there is no one perfect thing. Many of you might be thinking that you should have a strict diet plan and go to the gym to stay fit. Well, if you want to just go for it, going to the gym is the most awesome thing you can do. But, don't just sit somewhere thinking that you can't be fit. Just take one step at a time to make yourself fit. And I assure you, if you continue doing it, time teaches you to move forward and reach a goal that you have never imagined. You might think, Where the hell is Mufasa in the story? Well, he was with me throughout the journey. Whenever I felt like giving up, he was the one who pushed me to continue doing what I believed, in this story, something that I believed was to get strong and fit. You might also think that my belief has changed, however, I quit going to the gym, and I didn't listen to my Mufasa. Well, I always believed in staying fit till the last breath. Going to the gym is not the only thing that keeps me fit. As my Mufasa grew, he evolved, and his ideas towards what he believes in get better every single day, which made me who I am today. As days pass, I might be doing some other things to keep myself healthy, well, I might even start going back to the gym. But my 22-year-old self right now continues to do something for what he believes.

This was a long journey on my outer self, which is my body. The next story belongs to my heart, well, it doesn't belong anymore. This is the chapter of my life where I learnt and got hurt a lot, and let's get to it.

Chapter 3: Falling Apart

This was my second love, but this time it was a real woman. This is not a love story, it is a heartbreak one. People say that the emotional pain heals as time passes, and so does the physical pain. But the difference is that the emotional pain tears you apart from the inside out. You can't explain the way you suffer, there is nothing visible. It's just an endless volcanic eruption where the lava explodes inside and flows back to explode the same way or even more painfully again. It feels like an endless cycle of never-ending pain. Here, the distractions are just like covering up the volcano for a while until it gets strong enough to explode again. The more you try to cover it, the more pain it gives when it explodes. Now, let's get to the story.

Let's keep the love part aside, and let's just have her nameless in this entire story. This is the end of a 2-year-long story. The worst part of all this is that I had no clue that things were falling apart. The moment I realised, everything fell into fragments which could never be held back. It was the end of college, and that was the last time I saw her. After that, everything was going fine, or maybe it felt like it was going fine. Five months passed, and it was not as we were before. There were fewer fights and less speaking. It was like a smooth sail in a relationship, and one day it all fell apart like nothing. We fought I was the one who started the fight. Then, we didn't speak for some days. After a few days, when I spoke with her, she told me that she was confused. I had no clue what was wrong with her. She just started to ignore me, and one day, she said that she doesn't love me anymore and said that we should be good friends from then on. I asked for the reason, and she said nothing. I tried to know the reason, but she never told me any reason for that. And then, after a few long days of trying to fix it, I just gave up. I just became tired of her discrimination against me, trying to push me away. And I felt that I should respect her decision, and it would make her happier. So, I just agreed to let her go. It was hard to lose someone very close to your heart without even knowing the reason they left. Even this time, I tried to distract myself, but I couldn't; the pain just overcame the distraction. You remember something I told you about losing Kemo, this pain was 10 times harder than that one. My heart would just become too heavy for a few seconds for no reason. At that time, I had no one to speak with, I had to carry everything wherever I went. The nights were the hardest, I couldn't sleep well at night; every single memory of her would haunt me like there was no tomorrow without her. I even skipped working out on a lot of days. Then, days passed and I got a job, moved to a new place and got some people to speak with. I then realised why people move places when they are depressed, it'll just keep you busy with a new set of problems.

One of those major problems is food. If you want to eat healthy, you'll have to cook for yourself, I'll have to think about what I should be cooking every day in the morning and at night. More than that, cooking helped me focus on my thoughts. Then I felt that distraction was not a choice anymore, that is when I started to feel the pain inside of me. Whenever I felt the pain of losing her, I would just sit still and think deeper and feel more pain. It was hard at first, but as time passed, I felt my Mufasa getting stronger and stronger. The deeper I went, the less I became vulnerable to the same sort of pain again. Even if I felt the same sort of pain, it would hit me less hard. As days passed, I started to get back to my workout routine and my sleep. Everything felt like it was going fine. I felt like I was bringing the fallen pieces together day by day.

It had been almost five months since the day she left me. It was around 5:30 in the morning, I got a call, and the person said that she had left her house for another guy. And I also heard that they had been married 2 months before that day, and the tragic part is no one knew it until that day. I could not believe it at first, but as time passed, things started to make me realise that she went with another guy. I felt nothing, literally nothing, for half an hour; my mind was just blank, and I had no emotions for that half an hour, and after that, my hands started to shiver, and my heart started to beat fast enough that it was about to explode. I had to spend the entire day roaming like a sloth in my workplace. The day felt like the love I gave to her was for nothing. And I felt like I was a piece of shit. Well, that day was a complete trauma to me, and it was a completely different experience from the rest of my life. I just held myself till evening, and after that I took my bike, drove 40 kilometres to meet some of my friends to feel better. I just told them about what happened. As any other friend would do, they just started to give me some advice to make me feel better. But nothing made me feel better, except the fact that I felt less pain as I was in the company of some people around me. It made me feel better at the moment, but when everyone went away, the pain started to come back gradually. Even this time, for the entire day, not even a single drop of tears came out of my eyes. I wanted to cry like a baby, but I couldn't. Not just because there were people around me. My heart felt like it was too heavy, which didn't even let me cry. It was already late at night. So, I just stayed at one of my friends' houses. I tried to sleep, but I couldn't. Whenever I closed my eyes, her face started to come in front of my eyes, and my brain just started to rewind all the memories of her with me. I just spent the entire night without sleep. I was just lying still for the entire night with my eyes closed, hoping that I would get to sleep soon, but I couldn't. It was almost four in the morning. I just became tired of fighting myself trying to sleep. Then I realised it is better to sit in the darkness than try to sleep. So, I just sat in my dark room staring at my ceiling for about an hour. My brain was out of my control, it was just putting in random thoughts. I felt as if I was emotionally too weak, and I felt the Scar in me getting stronger as time passed. It was 5 in the morning, I just felt like speaking with someone., So, I just called a friend of mine. Thankfully, she picked up the call, I just started to blabber like a 5-year-old child. As I was blabbering, I started to cry, my crying never stopped for 2 hours. But once it stopped, I felt somewhat better. Then, as time passed, the pain started to get even higher. I felt like I was in an uncomfortable place where I couldn't be myself. So, I just drove back to my place and on my way back, I just realized that "I'll have to go through this myself and I also realized that no one could entirely help me on this and even if they do help, they couldn't be with me whenever I feel sad".

After reaching my place, I went for a walk, and I was determined to focus on the pain. Once I started to focus on the pain, I could physically feel like my chest was getting stabbed with a knife. The deeper I got, the more I felt the pain in my chest. But the pain felt different,

I was able to feel my Mufasa in that pain. And at that moment, I realised that "Wounds hurt the most when they start to heal". Even that night, I couldn't sleep, but I had a semi-clear vision of what I should be doing to keep myself mentally strong.

Days passed, I was kind of in a depressed state, every day felt like I was alone, but I had a hope that the days could get better sooner. Not just that, I also started to hate every woman for what happened to me. I didn't speak with anyone for a few days. Some days felt fine, and some other days were a nightmare. Also, I spent some nights with less than disturbed sleep. Mornings felt like my head was too heavy. Not just mentally, Day by day, I also started to feel physically weaker.

In the beginning, I started to blame everything on me, and I was just having a mindset that true love doesn't exist. And I even felt jealous, angry and bad about myself that I was not worthy to be loved anymore. Then, I just thought that I should not degrade myself for something that was not under my control. I then started to make my inner self stronger to fight her thoughts in me.

Now, while I'm writing this, it's been 3 months since she left for another guy. I still feel the pain that she left me, but it is not as it was a month before. Every day, I start to feel better about myself. Things that gave me pain in the past don't make me worry these days. And not just that, the Mufasa in me feels like he is stronger than ever. Every day, I could feel him getting stronger, not just to fight this pain, but it also gives a clear vision of what happens around me. Just because I feel less pain doesn't mean that I just moved out of it; I still feel bad some days, but the way I handle those things has started to change. And I am sure that I'm on my way to seeing this situation as just a piece of cake in the future.

Just because she left me doesn't make her a bad woman. She did what felt right to her, and I don't want to tell that she cheated on me. Because I don't know everything that happened, and just claiming that she cheated on me with what I am seeing is never going to be a fair game. But what I could tell is the way I felt and the things I learned from her leaving me. And that is what I tried to do in this entire chapter. And if there is one thing I should say at the end of this chapter, "Rather than trying to distract, just fight back your pain, even if you couldn't fight the pain, at least try to stay with it," it gives you more pain, but it is worth it. Things do fall apart to get strong back again

Sooo...what's the point of all this

This is something written by a 22-year-old myself. When you read this, I might be older with a much stronger Mufasa than right now. Just because I get older and more aware doesn't mean that my 22-year-old self is a less knowledgeable one compared to my older self. There might be some stuff that I might need to learn back from the one right now, while I write this. Every one of these stories is just unique by itself and taught me different things about life. But everything has one thing in common, and it is "The Pain".

In each of these stories, my Mufasa got hurt and the way I treated it made him strong. And this point in life is where my Mufasa was vulnerable to Scar. The way we see the problem makes a drastic change to what the pain gives you. Even a little feed to your Scar could make the entire situation worse than it should be. So, the three of these stories come down to telling me that "Pain makes you strong".

But in the end, I just want to add a few words: "Pain makes you strong, if you feed the right lion inside of you".

Ooh, wait, it's almost the end, and I haven't introduced myself right. Well, the name of this 22-year-old guy is Sriharan, and if you are reading till this, I just want you to tell this one last thing, "Hakuuunaa Matataa for life".

BREAKING BARRIERS: A JOURNEY OF EMPOWERMENT AND UNWAVERING SUPPORT

ASHRA SINDHIKKAA M

The terms "women's rights" and "empowerment" have gained their significance through centuries of relentless struggles against societal norms that sought to confine women solely to domestic roles like being a wife and a cook. After all these years, despite progress, many people still strongly believe that women belong only in the kitchen. The only difference between now and then is, they use fancy words like women's role is to "nurture", "give birth" and "take care" of the family to hold on to their male dominancy over the women in their family. They don't realise that she is losing her identity, including her likes and dislikes, to live a life that somebody else wants her to live. And the funniest thing is they make her believe that's what she wants and nobody else is making her do it, and yet again justifies it by giving another name as "sacrifice". It's not something to be proud of if you're sacrificing more than others, or if you are the only one always sacrificing. It's being taken for granted, and they may not have realised it.

In our community, parents often marry off their daughters soon after school, and even if they start college, many end up getting married within a year or two and discontinue their studies. The prevailing belief is that daughters will eventually marry, have children, and manage household duties, so further education is deemed unnecessary. Some even justify educating girls only up to secondary or high school so they can assist their children with homework. Even when some parents view their daughters solely in roles like cook, maid, wife, or Mom, it's challenging to shift societal perspectives to recognise that women can fulfil these roles and more.

Among those narrow-minded and conservative people, I feel fortunate and proud to have parents who value my independence even more than I do. In our generation, broad-minded is more common than decades ago, but my dad was a rare gem who shattered societal barriers even then. He worked hard by himself to become an auditor, and after marriage, he also encouraged my mom to pursue and complete her graduation. Years later, he surprised my mom by buying her a bike and teaching her to ride it, despite the societal belief that a woman can never ride a bike in the early 90s.

Despite the challenges, my parents continued to defy norms. Within a week, my mom learned to ride a bike in our colony. My Dad took it further, creating scenarios like forgetting an important file or needing to visit our grandparents to encourage her to drive independently. These challenges boosted her driving skills and confidence, just as my dad had hoped. Eventually, she became the first woman to ride a bike in our grandparents' area and among our family. Many viewed with admiration, especially envied by women, yet seen as unconventional by society at that time.

Unfortunately, in 2007, my mom met with a severe accident that left her bedridden for months with serious injuries to her legs and head. During this time, my brother and I stayed with relatives while my dad cared for her attentively, assisting with everything from bathing to feeding her like a newborn baby. The accident caused her post-traumatic stress, and she doubted whether she would ever ride a bike again. However, my dad was determined to make her believe in herself and bought a car for her as it's safer than the bike. Both my dad and brother encouraged, taught, and motivated her to learn how to drive it. Along with their encouragement and my mom's willpower, she once again started driving the car within months.

Many instances like these highlights the stark differences in our family compared to other conservative families. Observing the lifestyles and treatment of women in those households made me realise the harsh realities of society. Many women in those families yearned for independence and desired to be acknowledged for more than just their roles as cooks or servants, often labelled with the esteemed titles of "mom" or "wife". It was disheartening to witness men in those households ordering their wives or Moms to fetch food or water without even lifting a finger. They failed to recognise that managing household chores is physically demanding work that requires energy, similar to any other profession. They often fail to appreciate their wives or Moms, believing that providing food and shelter is sufficient. Their mindset disregards the possibility that women may desire more than necessities. What they overlook is that they are the ones determining what the women in their family can aspire to or desire.

When I was young, a relative proposed that I get engaged to their son, who was still in high school, with the idea of marrying him in the future. My parents declined, saying it was too early to make such decisions and that the age difference was significant. The relative reacted with anger and insult, claiming that since their son was destined to become a medical professional, I was missing out on a chance for a better life by not agreeing to the engagement. They belittled my potential. My brother was outraged by their disrespect and insisted that I needed to achieve something significant, like becoming an IAS officer, to prove them wrong. He emphasised that no one is inherently superior or inferior. Though I didn't fully grasp the situation at that young age, his words stayed with me, and I resolved to pursue a career as an IAS officer ever since. While everyone around me is aware of my ambition to become an IAS officer and has advised me to pursue a degree in arts to focus on IAS exam preparations, I was determined to pursue a distinctive degree in engineering or technology alongside my IAS preparations. However, societal pressures were relentless; marriage proposals began as early as eighth grade, with attempts to persuade my parents to marry me off quickly. There was a prevailing belief that daughters were burdens, and investing in their education, only for them to potentially become housewives, was a waste of money. Yet, these individuals were unaware of how deeply my dad cherished me right from the moment I was born. He distributed toffees to everyone when my brother was born, as he was a firstborn male, but he also surprised the entire hospital by distributing cake when I was born. Such gestures were uncommon then, given the prevailing mindset that daughters were financial liabilities and wouldn't care for their parents in old age.

I completed my schooling with biology as my major, as I already had a plan to pursue a Bachelor's of Technology in Biotechnology. Thanks to my good grades, I had several college options through Anna University Counselling, but only a few for Biotechnology in and around Coimbatore. Adding to the complexity, only one or two seats were allocated in each department for my community, further narrowing down my options. Despite having several choices for more common courses, I was determined to pursue a unique field and therefore opted for Biotechnology. So, then we chose BIT, as it stood out for its excellent infrastructure, facilities, and placement opportunities. On the other hand, I was also hesitant about staying in the college hostel, having never been away from home for more than a month, since it is located around 70-80 km from home.

During the admission process at BIT, these thoughts weighed heavily on my mind, but once again, my dad came to my rescue. He reassured me that I didn't have to stay in the hostel if I didn't want to. So, I opted to travel daily for a 30–40 minute journey to the college bus stop, followed by another 1 to 2 hours on the bus. I chose this commute over staying at the hostel because I didn't want to be away from home. My dad never complained or hesitated to pick me up and drop me off at the boarding point, even when he was busy with meetings. Meanwhile, my brother had gone abroad for higher studies, and couldn't support my dad with it. Some might perceive me as a spoiled or a dad's little princess, but let me clarify, I am also my mom's and my brother's little princess. They have always prioritised my happiness, a dedication that continues to this day, even though I am now married and living in another country away from them.

Due to long travel hours, I had to pause my IAS exam preparation and shift my focus to a career in my core field. I had always dreamed of working in Bangalore for reasons that remain unclear to me. By the end of my final year, that dream became a reality when I secured a position with a core company in Bangalore. I was thrilled about the opportunity to be independent and explore one of India's most vibrant cities, where my brother was also working. My entire family rallied to help with the move, and we all travelled together on a weekend to get everything settled before I started work on Monday.

My excitement and anticipation quickly turned to disappointment upon arriving at our new location. Although it was technically within Bangalore's jurisdiction, it was situated near the Pune border and bore little resemblance to the bustling city I had imagined. The area was remote, with no houses or hostels within a 3 km radius of the company, largely due to frequent incidents of harassment. After an exhaustive search, my friend (who was also set to join the company on Monday) and I finally found a place to rent about 4 kilometres away. The locals warned us about the dangers of two girls staying alone in the area. Determined to experience a new environment and gain financial independence, we decided to stay. On our first day at work, everything seemed normal until we tried to head home in the evening. We struggled for two hours to get an auto or cab, as drivers were hesitant to venture into the area due to safety concerns. Once we finally managed to get a cab and make it back, we reflected on the situation and decided that it wasn't worth the risk. The very next day, we packed up and returned home.

I felt lost and disheartened, unsure of my next steps, especially as I saw my cousins getting married right after high school or while still in college. Despite this, my parents remained steadfast in their beliefs and decisions for me. Initially, I hadn't considered further education, but when my brother suggested it, it felt like the right path. I was accepted into a postgraduate program at KCT, just a kilometre away from home. In my family and community, it's uncommon for women to drive, but my family, particularly my brother, encouraged me to break that norm. He not only taught me to ride bikes and cars but insisted I do so, stressing that it was a basic skill and I shouldn't depend on others. His constant reminders about self-reliance made me appreciate its importance later on. Eventually, I earned licenses for both two-wheelers and four-wheelers, enabling me to commute to college on my bike. To my delight, some of my closest friends from BIT also decided to join KCT, and what started as a solitary endeavour became a shared experience, making it all the more fulfilling.

At BIT, most of my friends were hostellers, so we didn't get to plan outings, but we created countless memories right on campus. At KCT, I not only reconnected with old friends but also made new ones. The hostellers had the freedom to stay out until curfew, so we often made spontaneous plans after college hours, occasionally even skipping classes for mall trips or other adventures. Interestingly, I always made sure to inform my parents whenever I skipped class, while my friends kept it from theirs. My parents believed in balancing studies with enjoyment, so they never objected to any impromptu outings or trips. Our dad frequently took us on vacations during school breaks, even during weekends, and we went out somewhere, exploring different parts of India. My mom is the kind of parent everyone wishes for; instead of pressuring us to study, she always emphasised the importance of health over grades. She never hesitated to celebrate our academic achievements, but also encouraged us to take breaks and prioritise our well-being. If I ever felt like skipping school or work, she would be genuinely excited for me to have a day off. Even when I asked her to wake me up from a nap while studying, she would let me sleep, believing that rest was more important than grades. My parents have always trusted me completely and never imposed their expectations. In return, I wanted nothing more than to make them proud and never disappoint them. Their unwavering support and, in my final year of post-graduation, our class advisor invited us to attend a pre-placement talk by a multinational company with a specialised biotech division. Although their focus was primarily on undergraduate placements, a few of us, including me, decided to participate in their recruitment drive for the exposure. To my surprise, they hired three students from our department, including me, and I was the only post-graduate selected. The company, a Bio-IT firm based in Bangalore, offered an impressive salary, and we were eagerly awaiting our offer letters.

While we were waiting, I discovered a professor vacancy at BIT. Although all my friends applied for it, I initially chose not to, as I already had an exciting offer in a city I wanted to explore. When I mentioned this opportunity to my mom, she encouraged me to apply to gain experience with a teaching recruitment process, which was different from the interviews I had attended before. Following her advice, I applied and went through the interview rounds.

After four rounds of interviews, I was chosen as one of the top six candidates out of fifty. However, none of my friends who had applied with me were selected, and I felt a sense of guilt being the only one among them who hadn't initially planned to apply.

I've always had a passion for teaching, even as a child. One of my favourite games was teaching my imaginary students with a board (that I had my parents buy for me) in my room during middle school. This playful approach helped me grasp concepts more deeply, and I often found teaching myself rather than studying even till Post graduation. However, I never considered myself a teacher or professor in an Educational Institution until the moment I received a job offer to become a professor. That call was one of the happiest moments of my life, surpassing even the joy of being selected by a Bio-IT company. It was then that I realised teaching was my true passion. Despite the Bio-IT role aligning with my dreams, I chose to follow my passion for teaching. When I shared my decision with my family, they weren't surprised, they had always known how much I loved teaching. Their pride and support, especially seeing my dad enthusiastically share my qualifications and career with his friends, make me feel elated.

A few months later, as my parents began looking for a suitable alliance, one major expectation was that my future husband and his family should allow me to work after marriage. However, I found myself questioning why I needed their permission to continue working. Isn't it my choice, given that I'm the one who will be working? I would be grateful for support in pursuing my career, but I believe that the decision to work should be mine to make, even in the future, based on the circumstances, rather than requiring approval from others. It was disheartening to confront the reality that women's life decisions are often dictated by others, much like a puppet or a role-play game. Many of the proposals I received insisted that I stay at home, with some even suggesting, "We don't rely on women for financial support, so she doesn't need to work," implying that my parents should be embarrassed about my career aspirations. This perspective is troubling. My father is well-established and has never depended on my income. I work because I'm qualified, I want to use my skills and be independent. What's there to be ashamed of about that? My family and I take pride in my achievements, which is what truly matters. Additionally, why shouldn't a woman be able to contribute financially to her family? Supporting one's family through work should be seen as a positive contribution or responsibility, just as it is for men. Similarly, if some women choose not to work, that is their personal decision and should be respected as such.

My family and I were perfectly fine with a groom having just one degree or a diploma, but this wasn't always the case for the groom and his family. Why is there an expectation that a husband must have superior educational qualifications and a higher salary than his wife? Education should be about personal growth and knowledge, not a competition to see who has more. In our community, having a college degree is now quite common, but obtaining a Master's degree remains rare. Many families of grooms often prefer partners who have only completed undergraduate or currently pursuing college, and it's not uncommon for these individuals to stop their studies after marriage. In this context, we were not considered by many prospective grooms simply because I hold a postgraduate degree, which some viewed as intimidating or inferior. To add to this, I was also pursuing a part-time Ph.D. This perspective assumes that women should always be in a subordinate position and are not expected to feel insecure or inferior, unlike men. What drives this need for one partner to be seen as superior to the other? Achievements like holding a degree or earning a high salary do not necessarily equate to maturity or true education. True maturity involves recognising that every individual deserves equal respect, regardless of gender, educational background, or socioeconomic status.

I believe that the ideologies and principles people follow are shaped by their upbringing and circumstances. In our home, even though my parents are the eldest, they have always valued and considered the opinions of my brother and me, starting from a young age. They listen to us, even when making important decisions, without letting pride get in the way. Our family discussions involve everyone, and most decisions are made collaboratively. Despite the distance, my parents continue to reach out to me for my input before making any decisions. Even when my parents sometimes forget to inform me of important details, my brother always keeps me updated. We share a close bond, with him guiding me through each stage of my life. He's not just a brother but a best friend who supports my decisions, even when they go against my parents' choices, recognising that everyone, including them, can make mistakes. At the same time, he helps me see my errors instead of just offering blind support. I plan to carry forward this practice in my own family, involving my husband and our children in important discussions and decisions, just as my parents did with us.

After a long search, we finally found someone who values and respects me for who I am, including my qualifications and career. My in-laws and husband are as proud of my achievements as my parents are. My husband, in particular, shares my views and doesn't compare our educational backgrounds. I am confident that he will be supportive and even more proud if I earn more than he does, unlike some of the less mature individuals I've encountered. My in-laws have been incredibly supportive and enthusiastic about my career. They encouraged me to continue working and pursuing my goals, which made me feel like I gained another family in them. Previously, I had planned to complete my Ph.D. even after marriage, assuming I would marry someone in Tamil Nadu. However, destiny brought my soulmate from another country. Despite this, he assured me that he would fully support my decision to stay in India and finish my Ph.D., which would take an additional three years, and that I could join him in Dubai afterwards. Just like my parents, he left the choice to me. After careful consideration, I decided to take a break from my Ph.D. for now, move to Dubai with him, and plan to continue my studies in the future. He has been supportive of this decision as well, just like I expected him to be.

One of the main reasons for my decision was that being apart for three years after marriage felt like losing precious time, especially during the newlywed phase. The little moments and special occasions that come with starting a life together are irreplaceable and fleeting. While my career is important to me, being with someone who values and accepts me as I am takes precedence. After moving to Dubai, I took a break and began looking for jobs in the teaching field to continue pursuing my passion. However,

I soon discovered that a B.Ed. was now mandatory for teaching positions in schools, a requirement that had been introduced just before my arrival. Previously, schools would hire UG and PG graduates for teaching roles. Unaware of this new requirement, I had spent months applying only to schools. When I learned about the new regulation, I felt disheartened and unsure of my next steps. I was eager to work because staying at home felt unusual to me, having always been engaged with studies or work. I then began applying for various administrative positions, but I received no responses. Despite having administrative experience from my previous role as a professor, my major background in teaching seemed to overshadow my suitability for these roles. Additionally, my postgraduate degree was viewed as overqualification for the positions I was applying for.

Deep down, I hoped to find a teaching position, as the career path I chose now will shape my future. Fortunately, I later found openings at various institutes, which renewed my hope. Throughout this process, my husband and in-laws were incredibly supportive of my determination to return to teaching. After a few months of searching, I secured a position at a training institute. The reactions from my parents and in-laws were truly heartwarming. I expected my parents and husband to be thrilled, but I was pleasantly surprised by the excitement from my in-laws as well. My father-in-law, in particular, was a great source of comfort during times when I felt discouraged by the lack of responses. What was even more remarkable was how my husband frequently checks in to see if I am happy with my current role. Even if I said I was content, he reassured me that I could always resign and look for another job or choose to stay at home, with his full support. Indeed, I am truly happy with my new job because it allows me to continue teaching. I wouldn't have felt as fulfilled in a different field, but I would have taken a job out of desperation.

I'm fortunate to have the support of two families who back my decisions and ambitions, despite societal challenges related to gender. Unfortunately, not everyone has the same level of support from their families when pursuing their dreams. While progress has been made compared to past generations, there's still a long way to go. I believe that with time, more people will adopt a broader mindset. I'm committed to passing on the values I've learned from my parents to my children. I want to nurture the belief in equal respect and freedom for everyone to make their own choices and live their lives as they wish, regardless of their gender. I hope others will embrace this perspective as well, since "change starts from within".

DREAMS / LOVE BEYOND BOUNDARIES

DR. MANJULA M

Manju was born in Tamil Nadu's capital, Chennai city, as the middle child of three, with an elder brother and a younger sister. Despite their limited education, her father, who had completed only up to the eighth grade, worked as a helper at a leading newspaper publisher, while her mother, though illiterate, was a woman full of love and wisdom—their dream was to see their children achieve success through education. Determined to uplift their family, Manju's parents sacrificed everything to enrol their children in reputed schools, often struggling to pay the fees. There were times when her father considered transferring them to government schools, but her mother, resolute and strong-willed, insisted that education was the foundation of success. She even took on small jobs to help support the family.

Among the three children, Manju was the most ambitious, determined to change her family's fate. During her

SSLC exams, she aspired to continue in a prestigious matriculation school. Although her father initially hesitated due to financial constraints, Manju promised to achieve high marks, and when she passed with 89%, her father borrowed money to fulfil her dream.

However, as Manju entered her 11th grade, her parents began discussing marriage. They found a match for her named Mr.Thiru, a successful businessman, six years older, born in a prosperous family. Though he hadn't pursued much formal education, he had built a thriving business. Manju, initially reluctant, eventually agreed to the marriage, thinking it would relieve her father of the financial burden of her education. Thiru appeared kind, responsible, and supportive, and she hoped to convince him to allow her to continue her studies.

Once Manju completed her schooling, they decided to get her married to Thiru. So Manju decided to meet Thiru in person. They went for a one-day date to Queen of Hills, which is a romantic, cloudy and chill place to hang on with a loved one. Their first meeting happened at a bus stop where Manju was waiting for Thiru to pick her up. Manju likes long drives on the bike, hence it happened as such. The second she met him, her heart fell in love with him because he looked handsome, cool and very caring. They drove to a restaurant in Ooty to spend their time together. The place was surrounded by nice music, good ambience and few people. They spoke a lot about their likes and dislikes. As time passed by, Thiru asked Manju if she wanted any gifts, as it was their first meeting. With a heart full of longing, she expressed her desire to become a doctor, a dream she had set aside due to her circumstances. Thiru, seeing the passion in her eyes, simply said, "**Don't worry, I am there**."

After their confirmation, both families arranged their wedding, and they both happily tied the knot.

The next day of their marriage, Thiru took Manju and admitted her to a reputed college in the city. Manju was very happy about continuing her education. Thiru used to drop her off at college every day. Despite criticism from his relatives and friends, Thiru stood firm, prioritising Manju's education.

After completing her undergraduate studies, Manju faced pressure from both families to start a family. Yet, without consulting anyone, Thiru enrolled her in a postgraduate course at a reputed college. Manju was overjoyed by his unwavering support and dedication to her growth. Two years later, she completed her postgraduate degree, a milestone that filled her heart with happiness. But with increasing family pressure, she approached Thiru about having children. He gently encouraged her to pursue a career as a professor first, urging her not to let her education go to waste. Manju began working as an Assistant Professor in a well-known college.

Just as Manju felt ready to settle into family life, Thiru took another bold step—he enrolled her in a Ph.D program. This decision caused an uproar within their families, as everyone expected them to focus on starting a family. But Thiru was resolute, believing in the power of Manju's education. After joining the PhD program, Manju and Thiru agreed to start a family, with Manju promising she would complete her doctorate. Soon, she gave birth to a beautiful daughter, bringing immense joy to both families.

As the time for her thesis submission approached, Manju faced pressure to give up her studies, but Thiru stood by her side, reminding her of her promise. With his unwavering support, she completed her thesis and submitted it to the university. After 1.5 years of hard work, Manju's Ph.D public viva voce was finally scheduled. As the day approached, Thiru took on the role of primary caregiver, ensuring their two-year-old daughter was looked after so Manju could focus on preparing for her presentation. On the day of the viva, both families gathered at the university, filled with anticipation.

As Manju began her presentation, their daughter grew restless and started to cry. Without hesitation, Thiru took the child to the parking lot, comforting her in his arms so Manju could concentrate on her presentation. In the conference hall, Manju confidently defended her thesis, answering every question from the external examiner and audience with clarity and poise. After what seemed like an eternity, the examiner made the announcement: Manju had successfully earned her doctorate. From that moment on, she would be known as Dr. Manju. The room erupted in applause.

As the cheers filled the hall, Manju's eyes welled with tears of gratitude. A flood of memories rushed back—her first conversation with Thiru on their wedding night, when she had confided her impossible dream of becoming a doctor. And now, here she was, living that dream, all because of the unwavering support of her husband.

Overwhelmed with emotion, Manju searched the crowd for Thiru. She couldn't see him. Instinctively, she ran outside to the parking lot, where she found him gently rocking their daughter to sleep, his arms cradling her small body on his shoulder. Tears spilt from Manju's eyes as she rushed to him, throwing her arms around him in a tight embrace.

"**I love you**," she whispered, her voice thick with emotion.

Thiru smiled softly, knowing that together, they had turned an impossible dream into reality.

FOND MEMORIES TO CHERISH

SHAARON ANN DSILVA

My definition of Human Resource is that 'Every Human being is Resourceful!' Hailing from a Human Resources background, I believe that every person can make an impact on others life. One of them might be influencing you to be an extrovert, another one can teach you something new by sharing their life experiences, someone may possess a skill that you could adopt, another may have extraordinary expertise in some area, and one of them may be gifted with an inborn virtue like patience. Any such person could be the actual inspiration behind your success in life.

The Power that Nature Wields to Shape Memories

I love the 'Rain'. June marks the start of the monsoon season. Being a petrichor lover, June is the month I enjoy the most in India. Rain drops cling to the tips of leaves, puddles of rainwater can be seen everywhere, the city streets are flooded with water, the never-ending showers during the night give you a calm and peaceful sleep, and the sound of thunder, flashes of bright lightning and the sight of the sky after a storm becomes clearer. I am very lucky to be born in June and to get a chance to stay in my maternal home to enjoy the monsoon. I am so glad that I get to see more rain in the UAE recently than usual. However, the rains during April 2024 were enormous and affected the daily lives of many.

When I was young, I used to wonder why the water bodies in Kerala had a greenish shade, whereas the sea in Dubai is a bright shade of blue. Today, as I recite my prayers using blue and green candles, I understand the significance behind these two colours.

Warm Summer Memories

Summer vacations are equally enchanting. The holidays in my childhood were all about reading my favorite books sitting near a tree while enjoying the breeze, watering the garden, harvesting and distributing my home-grown veggies, picking my favorite mesmerizing yellow flowers, listening to the chirping of birds, catching butterflies and ladybugs, hunting for mushrooms, watching cricket tournaments, collecting bags of tamarind or mangoes, biking, and feeding chicks with their favorite worms and greens. The water that is stored in earthen pots holds a lot of flavour and quenches thirst on hot summer days. Not that I am a home buddy, but living close to nature will help you realize that it is better to live a simple life, where there are no big demands and you can remain stress-free, where it is usual to wake up early during summer to enjoy life to the fullest, unlike today's digital world. Life was so simple in the 80s when we appreciated and found happiness in all the small things that nature provides. This is what I miss. I long for these childhood memories.

Trips to Cherish

A college trip to Rameshwaram was mind-blowing. Rameshwaram is a famous pilgrimage destination with temples, ponds and beaches. A boat ride and a long walk on the island brought us to a beautiful destination where the sand was white and the water contained a collection of corals that were too beautiful to describe. These places are a must-visit, as there are just a handful that remain. The breeze blowing from one direction on the Pamban Bridge was mesmerising. It showed me the power of wind, and it gave me a sense of triumph. I wish I could smell the fragrance of the neem trees that we encountered during the trip. Till this day, I stop whenever I see a Neem tree to enjoy its smell.

A memorable day for me and my family was when my son was barely a month old, and we were travelling to Abu Dhabi, all set to witness the arrival of Pope Francis. We had a fantastic experience of being able to see our Pope Francis and get his blessings. The event was held in Zayed Stadium in Abu Dhabi on February 5th, 2019. I was able to attend the mass with my newborn baby. He is the lucky one who got the privilege of his first mass being celebrated by the Pope, with whom he shares his birthday, which is December 17th. It was that day when I realised that Christianity is not about being a catechist or being involved with prayer groups during your teenage and youth years. It is much more than that. Christianity is living a spiritual life of sacrifice, lending a helping hand to those in need, providing courage to those who have lost hope and much more.

The Beyoncé concert in 2009 was indeed a day to treasure. The vibes from the audience are something that you can never experience while watching a recorded program. Standing in between the crowd for hours was tiring, but the moment the opening number "I am a Single Lady" started to play, the crowd began to cheer, and at that instant, it felt like I was in a different world.

Dreams Come True

I am a fan of Mohanlal, but like any other Keralite, I cannot deny my liking towards Mammootty, especially when he plays the role of CBI Sethuraman Iyer. It was my dream come true to watch Mammootty arrive for his stage program in Abu Dhabi. We were waiting for almost 4 hours, and it was a very cold and windy day. Beside me was my CEO, who is from Lebanon. He was equally excited to see Mammootty and wanted to know more about this talented actor. There was silence among the crowd when Mammootty arrived backstage in a helicopter accompanied by a few other artists.

Also, watching Shah Rukh Khan doing a promo in Dubai was another great experience. I was breathless as the crowd kept cheering to see the very famous SRK. SRK is such a down-to-earth person.

My Family

My mother is the architect of my life. Losing my mom was the worst thing that could happen to me. A mom's love is the purest form of love that you can never get from elsewhere. All that will remain after your mom is gone is her love and every single word that she uttered for your well-being. My mom's charming laughter, her voice, and golden words will remain forever in my thoughts and memory. I found a note from my mom a few days after she left us, which said, 'Pray Daily'.

My sister has always been my source of courage at any point in time. She patiently listens to all my wailing and gives me the courage to move on, no matter what the situation is. Her smile resembles and reminds me of my mom. A sister is truly a blessing after your mom.

My father is a very silent person, but he is a man with a lot of patience and strong willpower. Daddy was the one who insisted that I should complete my post-graduation before I took up a job. He was the only one who inspired me to take driving classes even before I started working.

It was when I met my husband that I believed in 'love at first sight'. He is a huge bank of patience. Every little gesture from him was interesting, and I was gobsmacked. We are imperfectly impeccable, and through the ups and downs in life, we have grown up stronger than before. Since our marriage, I have been blessed with an equally pious and loving family. It was exactly the family that I had wished for in my dreams. The biggest highlight in my husband's home is the scenic beauty.

I once had to stay in the hospital for a week after undergoing unexpected surgery. Leaving an 8-month-old baby and an 8-year-old boy and going in for surgery is very disturbing. All that you see in that state of hallucination is the innocent face of your little ones. My in-laws were not able to travel or support me during this difficult time due to the floods that were very common in Kerala during those years. The roads were blocked for weeks together until the rains subsided, which made it so tough for many people to travel during the monsoon season. My husband was the only person who was with me during the surgery and for the days I spent in the hospital. He was my greatest support during this time. My father & my sister along with her family took great care of my kids during those days, which was the greatest relief for me, getting an update from my sister on how the kids were doing and the feeling of satisfaction that I get after speaking to my loved ones or rather listening to them and silently humming, as I was advised not to speak much for a few days, was greater than any pain reliever I got from the doctor.

I also truly value the timely and priceless advice from my father-in-law and the infinite solutions my mother-in-law provides to any problem that arises.

Believe that Things Will Go as Planned

Once we had planned a trip to India to meet my sister and her family before they flew off to Canada. We had so many trips arranged, including a pilgrimage. My son's passport was due for renewal, and we started the process on time. However, the passport was delayed for a few weeks. At that point, it looked like we would have to postpone the trip, which meant that we would have to alter all our plans. Although I made several follow-ups for the passport, it failed. During this, I fell ill and had to take a rest. With only 2 days left to leave for our trip, I gathered all my courage and went to the consulate in Dubai on the last day before the weekend. Things seemed so difficult as there was a huge crowd at the consulate that morning at 7 AM. I waited and waited till it was 11. Then, I started approaching the officers one after the other after hours of waiting in long queues. At last, I reached an officer who patiently heard my whole story and understood my urgency. Within 5 minutes, I was granted permission, and one of the officers personally started searching for my son's passport. In another 30 minutes, we were granted the passport. I thanked the officer and happily left the consulate, as my travel plans were not in vain.

My mother had a similar situation in 2008 when her passport was not returned on time after visa stamping. On the previous day of travel, my mom went to the immigration officer. She was granted permission to speak to the chief. The officer took my mother along with him to his chamber, and they started searching rack after rack for her passport. The passport was wrongly placed in a different slot by one of the officials. My mom was thrilled to get her passport right in time for their trip.

HR Experiences to Recall

One evening, I had the worst experience of my life when I was called by the Director of Finance & Business Support for an interrogation. He looked very serious when he spoke to me, and soon, the HR Director joined us. All eyes were on me, and I felt so weird. They calmly continued to ask me questions like: Where did this resume come from? Who was your contact person throughout the process? etc. There was a candidate who was applying for IT roles who ended up being recruited as a Room Attendant, as his resume was falsified to meet the purpose and get recruited. It came to light that a staff member took money pretending to give it to me as I was the primary contact for Recruitment, and in the same manner, he promised jobs to so many others in their hometown with the same intention. It was 3 hundred thousand in their currency. Little did I know that there was a whole racket behind this recruitment. The candidate was given his welcome money, which was a token amount for him to meet his needs before he received his salary. This was forcefully taken by a known person who asked him to pay a huge amount as a recruitment fee. The guy was informed that this sum was to be handed over to the

HR lady who carried out the Recruitment Process, who was none other than me.

Another incident took place way back in 2010 when I was recruiting for a Pastry Chef. We had a pool of candidates, and the one selected was the best among those who applied. The interview call went directly to a Bakery Section, and the candidate who was at the other end of the call performed extraordinarily well. He got selected and he arrived from his home country in a fortnight. To my horror, the candidate who arrived could not speak a word of English. I was unable to communicate with him or get any kind of information as to what happened. We called back on the same number. This time, another person at the bakery picked up the call, but the moment they realised the seriousness, they hung up and decided not to answer any more of my calls. It was a nightmare to send the candidate back to his hometown. He was in a hurry to start working, but dejectedly got deported back to his hometown. It was evident that the candidate played around the recruitment process by letting his supervisor attend the telephonic interview, which allowed him to get recruited and arrive in Abu Dhabi without even being able to say his name.

Another incident was when one of the staff members got terminated. He left the company in a rage and deliberately made a plan to get me in trouble. He made fake offer letters with my signature and promised to hire 3 of the staff from another company. He left the UAE when his visa was cancelled. However, the 3 people kept following up with me for their joining formalities. I had to say, "Sorry, but I don't know you!"

HR Experiences to Appreciate

Mother's Day always reminds me of our car wash guy, who was desperate when he found out that it was his mother's last day. She was terminally ill. He used to shed tears every single day, asking for help for his mother's treatment. He was explaining how critical her condition was. Sadly, a few months later, his mom left him for her heavenly abode. Even today, the guy smiles at me and thanks me for the little help that we provided by donating a small amount for the treatment of his mother.

I had a great time attending the 'Plant a Tree' program with Emirates Environmental Group. It took weeks of tremendous toil by our team. We managed to collect 150 kg worth of aluminium cans from almost everywhere, like the metro station, backyard, barren land, roadways, restaurants, etc. On the day of the planting, we went to Ajman as a team and there worked like farmers, ploughing the field, softening the soil and removing debris. Once we planted 7 trees, we bid farewell to them by placing a placard with our company's name.

Earlier in 2010, I got the opportunity to do a beach cleanup at Sir Bani Yas Island in Abu Dhabi. The whole gang was ready with their personal protective equipment on. There was media coverage too, as we collected 35 bags of garbage from the beach and its surrounding areas. The ride to the island was remarkable as the boat had a speed of 90km/hour.

The UAE has a lot of culture and heritage centers that one should visit. There are museums and heritage centers in all the Emirates that depict the trade that UAE used to do in ancient times like fishing, pearl diving & date farming.

The event was bee's knees. I got dressed up in a sari that matched my company's logo and represented my country's culture at the same time. You get to do all this working in a multinational company that actually gives much importance to varied culture & heritage. A camel ride in a sari is something that I would never dare to do again. Each event in UAE has a festive spirit, I would say.

Job fairs, university recruitment fairs, and exhibitions are events that I enjoy in the UAE. Each time, it is a unique experience, and you get to know more about the latest technology. I encourage everyone to attend the same and share their knowledge and experiences with those who do not get a chance to attend such events. COP 28 was one such event that took place in Dubai in December 2023. Sustainability and going back to traditional methods of farming and fishing culture caught my attention at the event.

The Reality of Life

The worst part of working abroad is that you must stay away from your parents. When you have little kids, it is a blessing that you have countless lovely mommies who take care of your kids either in the daycare or at your own home. We had a wide range of mommies from Kerala, Tamil Nadu, Karnataka, Gujarat & Sri Lanka taking care of my kids. Much love to all those who showered the kids with immense love.

You learn to embrace and enjoy your struggles and appreciate all that you have. Have a purpose in life. Have goals and focus on living a positive life. Contemplate that all troubles will disappear one day. I would like to conclude by saying that I believe every single battle can be won with prayer. All that you need is to hold on and gain the strength to endure the pain.

FUELLING THE FIRE: TURNING PASSION INTO A FULFILLING CAREER

RAJINIKANTH U

The Spark That Changed Everything

I still remember the hum of the machines, the endless spreadsheets, and the weight of the safety gear pressing against my skin. The petrochemical plant was a world of precision, efficiency, and control. Yet, amidst the towering pipelines and the deafening roar of the factory floor, I felt something was missing. Something essential. Something that made me feel alive.

Have you ever looked around and thought, *Is this it?* That's where I was. A career that looked great on paper, but left me feeling empty inside. I had done everything right—graduated, secured a stable job, and settled into a role that many would envy. But deep down, there was a whisper. A quiet, persistent voice asking: *What if?* And then, one day, an unexpected detour changed everything.

A Glimpse of a Different Future

It wasn't a dramatic moment. No sudden epiphany or life-altering event. Just a simple training session organised by the company—something most employees attended out of obligation rather than enthusiasm. I almost didn't go. But something told me to show up.

That training room was nothing like the plant. It was quiet, filled with discussion rather than the sound of machines. And the trainer—he wasn't just presenting slides. He was storytelling, bringing concepts to life in a way that made people sit up and listen. There was something magical about the way he spoke, how he held everyone's attention, how he **ignited curiosity rather than just delivering information**.

I found myself hanging on to every word. And then it hit me—I didn't just want to be in that room. I wanted to be the one at the front. I wanted to **teach, inspire, and unlock potential in others** the way he was doing.

That small flicker of realisation would soon become a raging fire.

The Golden Cage: Secure, Yet Stifling

But it wasn't so simple.

I had responsibilities. A good salary. A stable future. Walking away from it seemed reckless.

Who gives up a sure thing for a dream?

So, I tried to ignore it. I convinced myself that training could be a side passion, something I pursued in my free time. But the more I tried to silence the voice inside, the louder it got.

The long shifts stretched into eternity. The once-familiar hum of machinery started to feel suffocating. The work, though important, felt repetitive. I craved human connection, **real conversations, moments of growth, and transformation.**

And then, I remembered something.

Back in my college days, I loved presenting research papers. I had spoken at conferences, won competitions, and thrived in academic discussions. I had coached students for competitive exams, helping them develop their interview and management skills. I had felt **alive** doing those things.

Why had I ever stopped?

Because life happened. Because security was seductive. Because stepping into the unknown is terrifying.

But then, I realised something even more terrifying—**spending my life in a golden cage, knowing I had ignored my calling.**

Taking the Leap: From Fear to Freedom

I didn't quit overnight. I started small.

I immersed myself in training and development, attended workshops, studied instructional design, and learned about leadership coaching. I volunteered for training sessions on weekends, spoke at industry forums, and tested the waters wherever I could.

Every session, every interaction, **fuelled my fire**. I wasn't just sharing knowledge; I was **witnessing transformations**. People left my sessions thinking differently, questioning assumptions, and feeling empowered. That feeling? That was it. That was the thing I had been missing all along.

But leaping wasn't easy.

The fear of failure loomed large. Would I make enough money? Would I be any good at this? Would people take me seriously?

Doubt was my constant companion, but **passion was my fuel**. And passion, when persistent, finds a way.

The Roadblocks and the Resilience

My first open session was a disaster—only five people turned up, and two of them were my well-wishers. I stood there, looking at the empty seats, forcing myself to push through the session despite the disappointment. I remember sitting in my car afterwards, staring at the steering wheel, wondering if I had made a mistake.

But then, I reminded myself: **Every master was once a beginner.**

So, I studied harder. Learned from my mistakes. Tweaked my approach. And slowly, I improved. One session at a time. One breakthrough at a time.

Before the recognition came, my journey into training was filled with small wins and countless odds. From volunteering for sessions to slowly gaining confidence through each experience, I faced moments of doubt, but every small success reinforced my belief that I was on the right path. The turning point came when I received my first real recognition—the **"Best Young Trainer" award from ISTD**. It was the first tangible proof that my persistence was paying off. And then, the floodgates opened. More opportunities, bigger platforms, deeper impact.

I worked with industry leaders, developed behavioural competency models, and even received **global recognition from ATD for "Excellence in Training Practice."**

Each milestone wasn't just an achievement—it was **validation that passion, when pursued relentlessly, leads to purpose.** Another defining moment in my journey was earning my ICF-ACC Executive Coach credential, a true feather in my cap. This certification wasn't just a recognition—it was a commitment to guiding individuals on a deeper, transformational journey, helping them unlock their full potential.

The Fire That Never Goes Out

Today, as a Group Head of Talent Management & L&D, I am no longer just training—I am **building learning ecosystems**, developing future leaders, and shaping the **way organisations think about growth and development.** Achieving my dream position as a The Chief Learning Officer (CLO) was a defining milestone, a testament to the journey filled with perseverance, learning, and the courage to embrace change.

But more than titles and roles, what truly fuels me is this:

- Seeing someone walk into a session unsure of themselves and leave with **confidence and clarity.**
- Watching individuals **discover their hidden potential** and use it to transform their careers.

- Creating **a ripple effect**, where one empowered person goes on to empower others. My mission is no longer about just career success—it's about **impacting 100,000 lives.**

It's about showing people that they are **not stuck**—that passion and purpose, when pursued with intention, can change everything.

Your Turn: What's Your Fire?

If you've read this far, maybe something inside you is stirring. Maybe you've felt stuck, wondering if there's something more for you out there.

Here's my message to you: **You don't have to have all the answers. You just have to take The first step.**

Maybe that means exploring a new interest, signing up for a class, or reconnecting with something you once loved but abandoned.

Start small. Take the risk. Embrace the unknown.

And remember—**your fire is waiting to be ignited.** The only question is: **Are you ready to light it?**

GRAB THE OPPORTUNITY

SUBAKEERTHI M

Everyone knows that the firstborn child is very special to their parents. We are going to read the interesting real-life story of a first-born child in Tamil Nadu (Sivaganga). She was born on Sunday (10th September 2000). The first female child for their family. Her family celebrated her birth like a festival in their village. She is growing up with a silver spoon up to her age of 9. After that, her family faced lots of economic issues. She is not a single child for their parents. She has two younger sisters. Their family depends upon her father. Her father never failed to make his daughters happy. He invested all his money in his daughter's education. Everyone asked in their village why you are wasting your money on your daughter's education, and think about your daughter's marriage. He replied, "Education is the only key to exposing themselves to the world". Look, his first three daughter are first in their school and college. Now they are Engineering graduates. His first-born child is an Agriculture engineer, and his second-born child is an Artificial Intelligence and Data Science Engineer and the third born (Kadaikutty Singam) is going to pursue Machine learning. Now the story is going to begin…

School life and College life:

She studied in Shri Ramana Vikass Higher Secondary School at Cholapuram, Sivangangai District. She studied very hard to make her father's dream come true. She got a good mark in her 10th and 12th grades. With their Parents and Uncle's (Father's Brother, Mr. Senthilkumar) help, she decided to join in B.E. (Agriculture Engineering) Bannari Amman Institute of Technology at Sathyamangalam, Erode District. She is going to the hostel for the first time in her life. She faced anxiety for the first three months of her college life. With her family's support, she continued her college studies. After that, her college hostel days became her lifetime memories. She has 8 friends in her hostel room from the Agri, IT & Food tech department. They made her college life colourful. Everyone knew college life was the best part of life. In college, the first year is filled with books and exams. Second year, they have that senior feeling to rag our juniors. Third year, they have OD for the presentations in other colleges. They spent that OD 25% for presentations remaining

75% on eating food in the food courts. In the final year done with the projects and the placements started.

First Job Experience:

She got her first job when she was in the third year of college. But it was not a successful career in her life. She discontinued her first job too early. After that, she lost respect in the family. Her grandfather died in May 2021; at that time, she realised the meaning of life. Due to corona her sister came from Dubai to India with her daughter and son. She used to teach her sister's child. Her sister asked her to come to Dubai along with them to search for a job and teach her child. She arrived in Dubai on 17th October 2021. Her Brother-in-law (Mr. Baskaran) and sister (Mrs. Jeevitha Baskaran) helped her to search for a job in Dubai. She got her job in Dubai on 15th December 2021 with the help of her brother (Mr. Deepak). Her first job (Landscape Company) in Dubai was given and supported by her Well-wisher, Mr. Karthikeyan. He is a very good motivator in her life. She decided to be thankful to him for her whole life. She struggled with her first job in Dubai and learned lots of experience in one and a half years. Then she decided to switch companies for the good salary. She got the new job with double the salary of her previous company, and she started on 14th April 2023. Now she is working as a

Quantity Surveyor in a Leading Landscape company in Dubai (Thanks to the Director and Operation Manager). Her Name is Suba Keerthi Suppukkalai, Daughter of Mr. Suppukkalai and Mrs. Sethukkarasi Suppukkalai. Be brave and strong, when the god is decides to give you the opportunity, grab it. I grabbed that opportunity. Now I am a Quantity Surveyor, Ms. Subakeerthi Suppukkalai (B.E. Agriculture Engineering).

Be thankful for the person who is helping you in a difficult situation. I need to thank the most important people in my life (Mr. SenthilKumar & Mrs. Banupriya, Mr. Baskaran & Mrs. Jeevitha, Mr. Karthikeyan, Mr. Deepak, Ms. Harinee, Mr. Mohamed Sultan Faris, Mr. Yaser Arafath, Senthil Anna, Sadiq Anna and finally the biggest supporter, Mr. Nanthakumar) who allowed me to present my story (Thanks, Mr. Praveen Anna). Believe in yourself and trust that everything happens for a reason.

"Girl children are similar to God. Let them study as they wish. Let them grab the opportunity. Let them pursue their dreams. They will make you proud as I made my parents proud now."

JOURNEY TO SUCCESS: OVERCOMING ADVERSITY AND EMBRACING RESILIENCE

REEMA

Chapter 1: Beyond Borders: A Tale of Resilience, Integrity, and Triumph

Meera, a young woman from a peaceful small town in northern India, had big dreams for her future. She was ambitious and determined to leave her humble beginnings behind and pursue higher education in the bustling city of Bangalore. However, Meera soon realised that her journey would be challenging.

As she began college, Meera confronted a daunting hurdle—transitioning from a science background to the intricate accounting world, a pivotal aspect of her MBA curriculum. The sudden shift in discipline left her feeling like a fish out of water, and she struggled to navigate the complex concepts and terminology that seemed foreign to her.

The language of numbers and financial equations seemed to dance tauntingly out of reach, casting a shadow of doubt over Meera's capabilities. Doubt whispered in her ear, urging her to retreat to the familiar shores of her previous academic pursuits. Yet, amidst the uncertainty, Meera found strength in her unwavering determination.

With grit and resilience as her guiding stars, Meera embarked on a journey of self-discovery, immersing herself in the world of accounting with relentless determination. Late nights were spent poring over textbooks, seeking clarity in the labyrinth of financial statements and balance sheets.

But it wasn't just the academic challenges that tested Meera's mettle. The demands of her MBA program and the pressures of adapting to a new city and culture weighed heavily on her shoulders. Yet, with each obstacle she encountered, Meera emerged stronger and more determined than before.

As she progressed into academia, Meera was tempted to compromise her values due to peer pressure. Her classmates tried to sway her from the path of righteousness, but Meera remained steadfast in her convictions and refused to give in to the wrong influences that threatened to tarnish her integrity.

Her refusal to participate in activities that went against her moral compass earned her the ire of her peers, who boycotted her in retaliation for her refusal to conform. Despite her hostility, Meera remained true to her principles, finding solace in her unwavering resolve and the support of a few steadfast friends who stood by her side.

Though the boycott weighed heavily on her spirit, Meera did not waver. She found strength in her beliefs and the knowledge that she was on the side of truth. Her resilience and integrity ultimately led her to triumph, as she achieved her goals and proved that staying true to oneself is always worth the struggle.

Despite the odds stacked against her, Meera refused to be confined by the limitations of her past. She embraced the challenges head-on, turning each setback into an opportunity for growth and self-improvement. Through perseverance and sheer determination, she began to conquer the once-daunting realm of accounting, one equation at a time.

As the years passed and Meera completed her MBA, she stood on the threshold of a new chapter in her life, her spirit unbroken and her dreams burning brighter. For

Meera, the journey from a small town in northern India to the bustling streets of Bangalore was not just a physical distance travelled but a testament to the resilience of the human spirit.

In recognition of her unwavering dedication and outstanding academic achievements, Meera was awarded a gold medal for excellence in studies. It was a testament to her perseverance, integrity, and steadfast commitment to excellence.

And as she looked ahead, Meera knew that no challenge could ever dim the fire of her dreams. She had faced adversity with unwavering courage and emerged victorious, a shining example of the power of resilience and determination.

Chapter Two: Embracing Family, Career, and Love

Meera's heart swelled with pride and gratitude as she stood adorned with the gold medal. It was a testament to her academic prowess, resilience, and unwavering dedication. However, amidst the jubilation, her thoughts turned to her family - the bedrock of her strength and the driving force behind her every endeavour.

Determined to share her success and provide opportunities for her loved ones, Meera invited her younger sister,

Ananya, to join her in the bustling city of Bangalore. With a heart filled with hope and excitement, Ananya embarked on her journey, guided by the beacon of her sister's unwavering support.

Together, Meera and Ananya forged a path of success, each drawing strength from the other as they navigated the challenges of the big city. United in their determination to build a better future, they leaned on each other through the highs and lows, their bond growing stronger with each passing day.

Amidst the hustle and bustle of their life, Meera achieved a significant milestone; she purchased her first house. It was a modest abode, a testament to her hard work and determination. Standing before the door of her new home, Meera felt a sense of pride and accomplishment wash over her. It symbolised her independence, a sanctuary she could call her own amidst the world's chaos.

As Meera focused on her burgeoning career and savoured the joys of homeownership, she was drawn to a kindred spirit - someone who shared her passion for life and mirrored her unwavering determination. Amidst the bustling cityscape amidst the cacophony of life's chaos, she found love.

Chapter Three: Navigating the Path to Love and Marriage

As Meera's love for her new partner grew stronger, she dreamed of a future filled with shared aspirations and cherished moments. However, the road to matrimony was full of obstacles that tested the strength of their bond. With her father passing away peacefully one night and her brother disinterested in offering support, Meera found herself navigating the intricate dance of wedding preparations alone. Regardless of the absence of familial support, she moved forward with determination, relying on her resilience and the unwavering support of her sister, Ananya.

Every detail of the wedding arrangements bore the imprint of Meera's unwavering resolve. She carefully planned every ceremony from selecting the venue to curating the guest list. Despite her challenges, Meera remained steadfast in her commitment to celebrating her love in a manner befitting her dreams.

On the wedding day, Meera looked stunning in her bridal attire, her heart beating fast with anticipation and apprehension. Entering the sacred bonds of matrimony was a moment she had eagerly awaited, but the absence of familial support cast a shadow over the joyous occasion.

But amidst the uncertainty, Meera found comfort in the love and support of her partner, who stood by her side as a source of strength and unwavering support. With each step down the aisle, Meera moved closer to a future filled with love, companionship, and shared aspirations.

As the wedding vows were exchanged and the sacred rituals performed, Meera felt a sense of tranquillity wash over her. In the eyes of her beloved, she found the promise of a future filled with love and endless possibilities. Together, they embarked on a new chapter of their lives, united in their commitment to face life's challenges hand in hand.

Although resistance from her family threatened to cast a shadow over their union, unexpectedly, someone from Meera's MBA program, who had been a significant mentor to her, showed up at the wedding and gave them blessings and encouragement. They reminded Meera and her partner that family is not only defined by blood but also by the bonds of love and connection forged through shared experiences. Meera felt grateful and renewed, and with the support of everyone who had touched their lives, they started their married life with hope, joy, and the promise of a future illuminated by the light of divine blessings and unexpected connections. Meera and her partner remained undeterred. Their love shone bright amidst the darkness, a beacon of hope and resilience in adversity.

Chapter Four: Trials, Tears, and Triumphs Across Continents

As Meera and her husband embarked on a new chapter of their lives in the Middle East, they faced unexpected challenges that tested their bond and faith. Despite the bustling city, they found comfort in each other while adapting to a foreign land. But soon, Meera received devastating news that broke her heart. Her younger sister Ananya was diagnosed with terminal cancer, leaving Meera feeling powerless and overwhelmed by emotions. Not long after, Meera learned that she was pregnant with her second child. This news brought both joy and sorrow as she struggled to balance her grief with the anticipation of a new life. Overwhelmed by responsibilities, Meera found strength in her husband's unwavering support during the darkest days. Together, they faced the challenges and uncertainty with determination and faith. As time passed, Meera's courage and resilience shone through the shadows of adversity. She learned that hope was her lifeline and that love would always triumph. With her indomitable spirit, Meera was determined to overcome obstacles, fortified by the love that bound her to her husband, sister, and unborn child. In the end, Meera emerged victorious from the trials and tribulations of life, discovering the true strength of her spirit and the boundless depths of her courage. She knew that no matter the challenges, she would face them with unwavering determination and the love surrounding her.

After the passing of her beloved sister, Meera was overcome with grief and despair. To cope with her loss, she immersed herself in her work and threw herself into it with an intense focus. The busy streets of Dubai provided a temporary respite, but she soon found herself confronting obstacles in the workplace due to deeply entrenched gender roles and biases. Nevertheless, Meera refused to let these challenges deter her from honouring her sister's memory and pursuing her ambitions. She persevered through the trials and tribulations of her professional journey, drawing strength from the memories she shared with her sister. Her resilience and determination ultimately led her to a newfound sense of purpose and triumph amidst grief. As she looked to the future, she knew her sister's love would continue shining brightly in her heart.

Chapter Five: A Test of Faith and Resilience

A few years after settling into their career, Meera and her husband received devastating news - their second child, a precious baby, had been diagnosed with leukaemia. The diagnosis was a sudden shock that shook the foundations of their world, leaving them reeling with disbelief and uncertainty. Despite the chaos and uncertainty, Meera refused to give in to despair. With her husband, elder son, and a strong support network from her employer by her side, she faced the daunting journey ahead with unwavering courage and determination. Together, they rallied around their ailing child, offering love, support, and tireless devotion in the face of adversity. From endless hospital visits to gruelling rounds of chemotherapy, Meera stood as a pillar of strength, guided by her steadfast faith through the darkest of nights. She discovered reserves of strength she never knew she possessed, facing new challenges each day with unbreakable resolve, drawing strength from the love that bound her family together. Through the tears and the pain, Meera remained a beacon of hope and resilience, her unwavering faith shining brightly amidst the shadows of despair. As the days turned into weeks and the weeks into months, their child's health began to improve, inch by precious inch. Though the journey was far from over, Meera faced the future with renewed determination and unshakable resolve, knowing that anything was possible with love, faith, and unwavering resilience.

In addition to her unwavering faith and resilience, Meera had also taken proactive steps to advance her career and education. She had acquired higher degrees and certifications, positioning herself as an expert in her field. She had also started networking within the HR fraternity, building relationships with industry leaders and professionals who could offer her invaluable insights and support. Meera's commitment to her career and her family was unwavering, even in the face of her child's illness. She worked tirelessly to balance her responsibilities at work and home, always making time for her family and ensuring that her child received the best possible care. Her dedication and hard work paid off, as she was recognised as a rising star in the HR community. Her colleagues and peers admired her strength, resilience, and unwavering commitment to excellence despite adversity. Through it all, Meera remained grounded, humble, and deeply grateful for the love and support of her family and friends. She always remembered what was truly important in life - the people she loved and the values that guided her actions. In the end, Meera emerged from her family's ordeal as a shining example of what is possible when we tap into our inner strength, resilience, and faith. Her story inspires and motivates those facing challenges and struggles, reminding us that anything is possible with love, trust, and unwavering determination.

Chapter Six: Rising Above Adversity

Amidst the turmoil of her child's illness, Meera found solace in the steadfast rhythm of her career. She embraced her work as both a distraction from the pain and a source of strength in the face of adversity. With unwavering determination, she immersed herself in her professional pursuits, refusing to let life's challenges derail her ambitions. Balancing her career's demands with motherhood's responsibilities, Meera embarked on a journey of resilience and determination. From the confines of the hospital room, she juggled conference calls and meetings, her unwavering focus undeterred by the chaos surrounding her. With each passing day, Meera's dedication and perseverance began to bear fruit as her career soared to new heights amidst the trials and tribulations of life. Despite her challenges, she remained steadfast in her pursuit of excellence, her unwavering resolve shining bright amidst the darkness.

MORE THAN A DREAM: MAKING IT REAL!

SARANYA BHADRAN

Introduction

It was a pleasant morning in Dubai.

As usual, I grabbed a glass of hot tea with medium sugar (I go for medium sugar to avoid my guilt of taking sugar) and sat on my sofa for a few minutes. Several thoughts in me, excitement and a bit nervous too. Guess what! I am going to attend my 'book launch' event today, wherein my story will be published too. This is indeed a dream come true.

You may have several ups and downs in life, but overcoming those and being able to stand brave and confident requires a lot of courage. Lots of learnings throughout the journey - about life, people, other people's lives, and whatnot.

So, today marks a milestone. A reward for all my hard work. An answer to many.

Now, if I spend more time on the sofa, I will be super late for the event. So, I pushed myself to get up from that cosy sofa, hit the shower, and take some extra time to get ready with the attire of makeup of my choice and satisfaction. I look at the mirror and approve myself before heading to an event, especially if the event is one for me to shine.

Sigh... Looking at my mirror, I approved myself 'I am beautiful, though my complexion is brown. I am confident, with all the struggles I have strived through. I approve myself; I love myself, "I love you".

Dear Readers, do you approve of yourself? Do you love yourself? If yes, have you ever told yourself by looking at a mirror, 'I Love You'? I doubt! Many of you have not... because it takes an effort to do so - organically, genuinely... It did take time for me! And here is my story:

My Story begins...

My childhood was not bad. I had a lot of fun, good loving parents, a loving sibling, good schooling, good neighbours, and a lot more. Can't complain. But was I confident? Did I approve myself? Not really! My childhood was in a small village named Mulluvila in Kollam district in God's own country, Kerala, in the most diverse country, India. In this small village, there were quite a lot of judgmental people around me. For everything I do in life, I have to get approval from others, and opinions used to pour in without even asking. A place where the success of your life was determined by others. Since my childhood, I always had this thought of moving away from my village, away from my State, to pursue my studies, to show people in my hometown that this isn't the definition of success, this isn't the way you treat women and women's dreams.

I was always bullied by schoolmates, neighbours, and relatives for my brown skin, protruding teeth, and my beauty. (Though they bullied, I still call it 'beauty' as the readers should also understand that one's beauty is not something to be determined or approved by others, but by yourself!). They say beauty lies in the eye of the beholder. But who is the beholder? It's you. Look in the mirror!

Some relatives used to bully, even stating, 'Please save loads of gold and money to get you a good groom'. It was all a joke for them, because little did they know about the trauma and scars they would leave on a child. While it was a trauma then, now it all seems to be like a hard push for me to strive, overcome, and excel in life. Before I speak more about success, I prefer to speak more about the process. I learned it the hard way.

During my school days, I could feel ignored and rejected. Guess how? Teachers used to indirectly reject you, and select the most good-looking girls to be on the dance floor, for speeches and other events. I was devastated many a time. But glad I could still overcome. Resilience at peak - I realise now. Kudos to me!

If I ever visited a temple, an event, a wedding function, a birthday party, whatever it is, there would have been at least one jerk who would speak of my skin colour and discredit me. I used to shy away with a smile, but deep inside, I had a lot of discouragement, a lot of dislikes for myself, and a lot of questions to God, asking why you even created me this way. Hmm... does this sound silly? Trust me, it wasn't silly then!

At some point, all these comments and jokes became a sense of encouragement to push myself to be 'someone' valued and respected in life. I then started my search for that 'someone'. Do you think I found her? Yes, I did!

School days, Teenage...

At the age of 13, like any other girl, I started experiencing love and infatuation. Had a crush on a few boys. None responded on a positive note - of course, me being me, society being the same society that looks for beauty. Again, those were sad days as you were surrounded by a lot of friends who always had successful crushes or love stories to share, and you were left with none.

During all these stages, one good thing I could hang on to was my studies. Never went below average in studies. Always been good at studies and determined to learn new things. School teachers never considered me to be an outstanding student for obvious reasons. Students who scored the highest marks used to be applauded and encouraged for more and more success. As we learned, 'Rich becomes richer and richer, poor becomes poorer and poorer'. At schools, bright students become brighter and brighter, and others go unnoticed and unmotivated. Sad truth!

After my 10th grade exam, the time when I grew more beauty-conscious, I grew my confidence too. Irrespective of others' opinions, I decided to pursue 'Commerce' in Grade 11. All around me discouraged me, stating 'Commerce group is for non-studious children and Science group is for studious children'. Seriously? I think even today, there are a lot of people unaware of a lot of job streams in which one can explore. There was a family friend who visited my home and tried convincing me stating the science group was the best, you need to be in that group to be a Doctor or Engineer. Just in case you don't become a Doctor or an Engineer, you can still decide on another stream just because you will be in the Science group. This didn't change my decision.

My quest for finding the above-mentioned 'someone' was underway. So, I suggested my parents send me out of Kerala for my Grade 11 and 12. They tried, but their financial status did not allow them to. Obviously, at that age, I was still adamant about going out of Kerala, irrespective of my parents' financial capability. I dreamt of studying in a hostel in Chennai/Ooty/Coimbatore/Delhi/Bangalore. It disappointed me as I dreamt of days when my neighbours and schoolmates approved of me just because I would have been different from them, and moved to a different city for studies, would have made new fancy friendships, would have had travel experiences - it was all a myth, I know. But then, those were my little daydreaming topics, and my thought process was so narrow. (Laughing at myself now...)

The dream of leaving Kerala to pursue Grades 11 and 12 was not realised. But, again with my resilience ability, I got rid of those thoughts, and happily, I pursued my studies in Commerce at the same school in Kollam. The number of students was few in this group, as the society always considered the Science group to be a status symbol. Absurd! While I respect everyone in all streams, I pity the ones who inject such wrong beliefs into children of that age.

Trust me! I never regretted even once in my life for not opting for the Science group. I had my best two years of studies in grades 11 and 12. Learned quite a lot about interesting subjects like Accountancy, Business Studies, Economics, etc. As I learned with a lot of passion, I scored the best marks in grade 12. This made my parents proud. Above all, it made me proud of myself.

College days..

Now was the time to again nudge my parents to send me out of Kerala for studies. While their financial status improved a bit, not good as to decide easily on higher studies outside Kerala. So, my push was needed. Right now, when I write this story, I have the maturity to think that it would have been so mean from my side to even push my parents to support me, even after knowing it wasn't easy for them to spend on studies outside Kerala. But again, the point is 'it all led to success, and I never let them down with their decision'. Tamil Nadu is the nearest the cheapest neighbouring State to send me. So, we started exploring colleges in Tamil Nadu. Narrowed down to Coimbatore, which is 8 hours by train from my small hometown.

Finally, it was another small dream come true. I got admitted to CMS College of Science and Commerce in Coimbatore. The BEST decision I ever made, for various reasons. With my hard work during my school days being a cadet at NCC, I could get a scholarship (fee discount) at college too. Being a cadet wasn't easy. I used to go for 10-day camps, be on some yucky diet, and under strict officers' training. But all that hard work was repaid when I went to the admission counter of CMS College, Coimbatore.

Even today, I would love to relive those days in CMS. I had my best days of my life in CMS. The first year, like any student, was with fear. College was then famous for ragging. Had sleepless nights, and used to feel homesick big time. But, I told myself, 'You wanted this, you got this. Now, you live through this.' Slowly got friends, and changed friends. Nothing changed much compared to school. In CMS college as well, I was never approved by all. I could feel the difference, the discrimination, just that it was a little better compared to the school. But during breaks, on my way to the college mess or cafeteria for lunch, my friends were noticed by Seniors, and used to get proposals, flowers, and letters. While my friends used to act scared, back in the hostel, there were things for them to brag about. And I had nothing much to brag about. At that age, it was a sad feeling; a girl would know. Are you a reader who can feel that, too?

My second year in college was amazing. I could witness love, breakups, friendships, cheating, etc. But this is the time when even classmates started learning and considering character over beauty. And there you go, girl!

I won hearts due to that. My confidence level changed. Not every girl would admit this. But in this book, I am admitting. Proposals, in addition to appreciation, were always a source of improvement in confidence and self-love. I made a lot of good friends. Travelled and gained experience.

In the third year of college, I experienced what love is. Experienced betrayal too. Had ups and downs. Emotional days were more. But felt better than those sad school days. Nevertheless, my college days at Coimbatore were awesome – the best days of my life. It was so disheartening to leave that college and friends. But it's life, and we need to move on. I joined another college in Tamil Nadu for an MBA. I never liked that college. I wanted my days in this college to end as soon as possible.

The only happy days were when I used to meet my friends, or visit Kerala for leave. During my MBA days, I got in touch with one of my friends who studied in Coimbatore, and we met in Thrissur, the cultural city of Kerala. It was a usual friends' meet-up. But the friendship grew to a different level. Started talking to him daily on the phone. He went to the UK for his studies, and I continued my studies in this least-liked college. I got a campus placement – initially, it was an internship in Chennai. Those were the days when our relationship grew into love. That was an amazing phase of life. The period in which 'both of you love each other, but never told each other'. It was a nice feeling – 'Is it love' feeling. I am still smiling and blushing, thinking of those beautiful days.

My internship was in Chennai, and I used to be at a paying guest home at Nandanam, Chennai. I used to go for a walk in the morning at around 5 AM, and a call came from him at the same time. It was all a sign of love. He was studying in the UK, and it was his odd hours, but he still made an effort to give me a call every morning. Slowly, it grew into a stronger relationship. We both informed our moms without much delay.

Later, to the whole family. He returned to India post his studies, and I moved to Dubai with my sister in search of a job. Fortunately, I found a job in HR – my passion. The initial days were difficult – new country, new rules, away from family, and most importantly, away from my love. Like any human being, I adapted to the new environment, and by then, he came to Dubai too.

We got engaged in a couple of years. Pre-wedding times in Dubai were great. Fights, patch-ups, love, and whatnot. Finally, we got married in the year 2015. We built our career by then – I would call it 'not bad'. Our hard work paid off, and we are still working hard.

We were blessed with a cute baby boy – God's gift!

With struggles and accomplishments, life went on. I took a career break post my delivery, but got back to work again after a year. I always had in my plans that I needed to buy a house for my parents in the small town, Kollam in Kerala. After a few years of hard work, I could afford and achieve this dream. I, with the help and support of my husband, too, bought a house in Kollam for my parents. This was one of the proudest moments in my life. The happiness I see in my parents is what makes me happy every day, too.

I am currently working as an HR Manager with a Fintech company in Dubai, a role I am passionate about. Accomplished a lot of things that I couldn't afford a few years back.

Now, this takes me back to those childhood days when my neighbours and relatives used to underestimate me, judge me, and label me. Irrespective of all insults, I have achieved what I wanted to.

A few days back, one of my family friends bought a house, and she messaged me stating 'Followed your path, you were an inspiration. This again filled my heart with content. When you know you were an inspiration to someone, What more does one need to be content? This is an answer to all those who labelled me.

Dream high, believe in yourself – **Dreams are not just to be dreamt; they are to be realised!**

Thank You Note:

Thanks to all those who stood by me – The Almighty, my family, my friends, and even the ones who had demotivated me, as that served as a push to do more, too. Cheers!

MY SPELLING BEE JOURNEY: FROM THE POINT OF VARSHITHA SUDHIR

VARSHITHA SUDHIR

Have you ever imagined winning a spelling bee? The thrill of a win from the Scripps National Spelling Bee can bring many benefits and exciting rewards, such as a trip to the White House, a chance to appear on the news, a cash prize of $50,000, and more. I am Varshitha Sudhir, and I want to share my personal experience so far as a participant in the spelling bee.

Participating in a spelling bee is no easy thing. It is an arduous and challenging task that requires a lot of hard work, dedication, preparation, and effort. As a participant, I tried to prepare myself for the competition by learning all the English language rules, and it also helped me to try and learn Greek and Latin roots. In my first year of spelling, when I was in fourth grade, I lost at the school bee, because I didn't know much then, and I was just trying to spell. But I didn't let that setback discourage me, and I worked hard to get farther than I did the next year than I did in my first year. When I heard that they would do the class spelling bee, I started to practice right away in the word club app and the list my teacher gave me the day before studying.

The day of the spelling bee was filled with a mix of nervousness and excitement. As I got out of the car, I could feel the cool breeze on my face and hear the sound of leaves rustling in the wind. I could also hear the sound of my parents wishing me luck for the bee. As I walked into the classroom, I could hear the sounds of other students chatting and laughing. As I waited for what seemed like an eternity for the spelling bee, my heart pounded so loudly that I could hear it in my ears throughout the day. I fidgeted in my seat and nervously tapped my foot on the ground.

Finally, when the time came, my heart raced as my teacher explained the rules of the bee. During that time, and the time before the bee, I was revisiting all the words on the list over and over again in my head until I made sure I knew all the words thoroughly so that when she asked me, I knew them at the top of my head. I could feel the sweat forming on my palms.

As I stood in line, waiting for my turn to spell. Once she finally explained the rules of the bee and answered any questions anyone had, she told everybody to line up in our number order. It went from number one to number twenty-eight. I got up from my desk and got up and stood near the end of the line, because I was number twenty-five, and I stood near twenty-eight. My teacher started from round one, on person one, and every time it was my turn to spell, my heart pounded with nervousness. One to two people got the words wrong in the first round, and I knew everybody was dreading the final: "I'm sorry, but that is incorrect." At the end of every time, they were done spelling the word, but I was confident I wouldn't hear that for me. Finally, when we were left with three people, the difficulty level went up the difficulty level. My friend who participated in the bee got the word wrong, but so did the other student, and I got the word correctly so I was asked to step to the side while my friend and my classmate competed against each other, and unfortunately my friend got the word wrong and my other classmate got the word right, and he was named second place champion while I was named first.

Once I got home, I was jittering with excitement to tell my parents. As soon as I entered the house, I found my parents in the living room. I could see the pride in their eyes as I told them what happened. They hugged me tightly, and I felt their warmth spreading through my body. They congratulated me and told me they were so happy that I could go to the school level, and this time, I was going to win it.

The next day after the classroom spelling bee, I won the spelling bee, and my teacher gave me a four-hundred-fifty-word list. The words on the list and the idea of having to study four hundred fifty words were daunting and scary at first, but I knew that later on, I would have it just as well memorised as the class bee spelling list. As soon as I got home, I showed my parents the list and I started to work on it right away. The first part of the list was fairly easy, for it had words like sky and screeched. The next part of the list was the hard part. It ranged from words like thorax to simultaneously. I had a week, and even though I didn't think that was enough time, I knew I was going to know the list from the very front to the back. A few days later, as I predicted, I managed to know the list inside and out as I did with the classroom spelling bee list. I used the last few days to revise and go through all the words to make sure that there was a chance that I could win.

On the day of the spelling bee, the sun was blazing, casting a bright glow on everything it touched, and the air was filled with the sweet fragrance of blooming flowers. As I walked through the gates of my school, I could hear the sound of my footsteps.

Echoing through the empty corridors. I felt a mix of excitement and nervousness as my parents gave me a warm hug and wished me luck. As I entered the Multi-Purpose Room, I could see the other contestants feeling the same way. The room was buzzing with excitement, and I could feel my heart racing as I took my seat in the first row. The sound of my classmates cheering for me echoed in my ears as I nervously waited for the spelling bee to begin. My palms were sweaty, and I kept biting my nails to calm my nerves.

When the first round started, I could hear my heart pounding in my ears. The judges' cards, held up to indicate whether I had spelt the word correctly or not, made a satisfying rustling sound as they flipped them over. When I got my first red card, my heart sank, and I could feel a lump forming in my throat. As the competition progressed, the tension in the room was high. The sound of pencils scratching on paper filled the air as the judges scribbled down their answers. I felt my heart racing, and my hands were trembling as I waited for my turn. Finally, when I got the word right and secured my second-place position, the joy and relief that flooded over me were indescribable. The sound of my classmates and parents cheering for me made my heart swell with pride, and the warmth of the medal around my neck made me feel like I had accomplished something truly special.

The level after the school spelling bee was the district. This time there was no list, so I assumed and was 89% sure the words from the Word Club app were going to be asked, but there were four thousand more words to study, including the word in the school bee study list. I studied the list, but unfortunately, I was not as thorough with this list as I was with the previous lists, so when the day of the bee was close by, I was nearly panicking.

When the day of the bee finally arrived, I was so nervous that my hands were shaking uncontrollably. I could feel my heart beating fast and my stomach churning with anxiety. As I made my way to the city centre, the sound of my footsteps echoed in the empty streets, adding to my nervousness. Once I reached the venue, I could smell the faint scent of freshly brewed coffee wafting through the air. The tables were neatly arranged, and the chairs were set up on the stage. I went up to a table and took my assigned number, feeling the smoothness of the plastic tag as I put it over my neck. As the contestants were asked to sit up on the stage, I could see my teacher and her daughter sitting in a chair watching me intently. I also caught a glimpse of my friend, who was sitting closer to the front, where I could see her better. Then, after a moment or two, there was a lady who told us to get up and she told us to follow her. We all did as we were told, and We walked around the room, stretching our arms and legs and getting ready to spell. I could hear the sound of my breathing as I tried to calm myself down. After a few minutes, we were asked to take a seat at our assigned seats with our numbers on them. Then once we were seated, we waited for a long time while the judges explained the rules, even though we already knew them because they had already been said multiple times at the previous rounds. Once everyone was clear with the rules, we started the bee on round one. I could feel my palms sweating as I waited for my turn. I was surprised to find out that the word they were giving me was on the school list! I was so happy, and every word that they gave me up to round thirteen, I got right. On round thirteen, with only three contestants left, including me, there was a word that I did not know, and I misspelt it. I could feel my heart sinking as I realised my mistake. In the next round, the contestant before me spelt the word correctly, meaning she would be named first place if she spelt the next champion word correctly. In the next round, the speller before me had spelt the word correctly, meaning she was given first place. Now it just left me and the other participant fighting for the role of second-place district-level bee champion. In the next round, after the speller in front of me won, I was given the word "cinematography", and I was so relieved to hear a word that I knew. I could feel my confidence returning as I spelt the word correctly. If I got the next champion word right, I would be in second place.

In the next round, I did get the word right, leaving me the second-place champion and the third-place winner the contestant after me. After the judges gave me and the other winners the medals, the participants were dismissed from the stage. I went and met my friends, family, and my teacher, who said they were all very proud and happy. I could feel a sense of accomplishment as I walked out of the venue, ready to take on the next level of the competition.

Even though I won the district spelling bee after studying the school list, I was sure the regionals required me to study words from the champion list, so I studied it. A week later, I studied the list, but I just realised that I was also supposed to study the vocabulary of the words the day before the bee, so I tried to study as much vocabulary as possible.

The next day, I walked nervously into the cool, quiet main office of my school to take my spelling test. The scent of freshly brewed coffee wafted through the air, and the sound of typing echoed in the background. The vice principal greeted me with a kind smile and led me to a small, dimly lit room with a computer. As I sat down, the hum of the computer filled my ears, and I felt the coolness of the metal keyboard under My fingertips. As the test began, my eyes scanned the screen, and I saw a few familiar words, but I also spotted several words I didn't recognise. With each word, I could feel my heart beating faster and faster. Then, after twenty-five words, the vocabulary section appeared. I read each word carefully, trying to recall its meanings from my study sessions. At the end of the test, I anxiously awaited my results. After waiting for the screen to load for a while, it showed me that I had scored a 30/50. I wasn't sure if this was a pass or a fail, and my mind raced with worry.

A few days later, I received my final results after finishing my tennis practice. My mom shared the news with me that I had not advanced to the next round, as I needed to score 44/50 to qualify. My heart sank, and disappointment washed over me. I spent the rest of the day in my room, sulking and thinking about what I could do better next time. I even started to study the 2024 words of the champion list, vowing to memorise every single one.

A few days later, after taking a break, I decided to start reading the words of the champions list again for next year. Then my dad came in and asked me if I wanted to go to a class with the coach who taught Dev Shah, the spelling bee winner last year. And I was A little shocked when he asked me that, because I didn't know that Dev

Shah even had a spelling bee coach. I said yes to that offer, and my dad signed me up for the class. A few days later, I found myself sitting in my chair in a Zoom meeting with Scott Remer, my new coach. He evaluated me, and I was put at a beginner level, which was not surprising.

Scott sent me an email explaining what I should do next, which was to study the words of the champion list 2020-2024, study his books, and memorise Spell It! And paideia.

I immediately started to study what he told me to for at least 1 hour each day. I set a daily goal for myself for vocabulary, words, and stems.

Participating in a spelling bee requires not only hard work and dedication but also courage and determination. It can be a challenging yet rewarding journey that tests your Knowledge, memory, and composure. However, with hard work, persistence, and a never-give-up attitude, success is achievable. Being in a spelling bee teaches you to push forward towards your goal, even in the face of daunting or difficult tasks. It instils in you the value of hard work and dedication and shows that one can achieve anything they set their mind to with the right mindset. So, take the plunge and embark on this exhilarating journey towards great heights!

PLUS, MINUS AND EQUAL

ANU RANJANI

"No matter where you are and what is going on in your life, a kid's smile will always find a way to furnish sunshine in your life." Imagine you are the reason for the smile, not just one but a gaggle. Especially when they are God's kids.

I was in the Rotaract club during college. I took active participation in social activities and events that came through, visited a lot of orphanages & old age homes, which gave me exorbitant happiness while being with them. It's not about how much you give but how much you're passionate about the service you do for them, all I could offer is a good variety of food, stationery and outfits and most importantly, a heartfelt presence with them,… Those sparkles in their eyes encourage me to work harder to be consistent in witnessing their priceless smile. I restarted welfare services in 2018, since then I have made sure to persistently participate & contribute to the best of my abilities.

> *"We make a living by what we get, but we make a life by what we give."*
>
> **– Winston Churchill**

I was always in love with kids and always felt in my element with them. This flourished more when I started to be that little helper of my granny to take care of my other 7 cousins, who grew up along with me in my grandparents' house during my childhood. And I took permanent residence there for more than 12 years, so it's always babies and toddlers around me, as my aunts were working mothers. My granny wanted to support them in their career, which is a great thing of realisation for me even now, because it's not easy to be the moral support for her kids and also be the primary care provider for her grandchildren as well. And she did it calmly with lots of love. She always used to tell us that she wanted to give the care and support that she never got in life because she lost her parents at a very young age, so she had to raise her 8 kids all alone with no support. She is the most inspiring woman in my life because whatever she does, be it cooking, managing finance, raising grandchildren or handling hard times, she does it with ease and poise. I haven't seen her complaining about anything and has carried an optimistic approach to everything.

But also, I felt pity for her because back then, womanhood was just cooking, doing household chores, raising kids, servicing their husbands, getting their kids married on time and taking care of their kids too. Her success or failure parameters were based on the above factors only. I would never see her sitting relaxed with the coffee or listening to her favourite radio channels, she either runs behind her kids or her grandchildren. Witnessing all this at a very young age, I was always fascinated by babies & all baby duties, and I strongly believe this trait was inherited from my granny. Eventually, my love towards babies and having one for myself has grown boundlessly.

Days passed by, entered adolescence with lots of fun and frolic as I had a beautiful environment with a lot of people around and was exceptionally pampered by everyone as I was the only constant grandchild who took that forever favourite place in my grandparents' house. Completed my graduation and post-graduation, I did my post-graduation in Sathyamangalam, which is far away from Coimbatore, my hometown. So, I had to be in a hostel for studies. After a point, I so badly wanted to be a day scholar for a few personal reasons and homesickness. But my parents didn't allow me to travel all alone every day, as my college sometimes demands to stay beyond 6 pm, and I would have to travel at odd times. So, they gave me to option either to discontinue the studies or be a hosteler for another year too. But my mindset during that time did not allow me to take any of the options, and I was adamant about the decision to be a day scholar and complete my studies. Meanwhile, I should give credit to the faculty of my department and the principal who contributed their time to me in counselling me, as they also found the danger in travelling during odd hours. After so many rivals and chaos, guess what my granny did? Yes, she was all prepared to rent a house and stay along with me in Sathyamangalam and was with me until I completed my studies, just to fulfil my wish. I was happy then because I always loved to stay with her, my parents would visit us on weekdays, or we would go to our place. But I also still regret that decision to put her in such a difficult situation at that age; she was definitely in her early 70s at that time. It's just us, our house, my bike and a life at the very unknown place. They taught me a lot of life lessons, which I am thankful for even now, with the regret of troubling her. I loved her company and we are like friends, she used to cook for me, remind me of projects, important assignments, gossip, and she is the greatest support I've ever had.

It's not flesh and blood but the heart which makes a nurturing mother and granddaughter. She is more than my mother to me, then and now. How powerful motherhood is; it doesn't come with conditions and expectations, it just wants the child to be happy. My Mother and grandmother have set a lot of examples of exceptionally good mothers and breaking the stereotype for child growth and happiness. I am blessed to have these two loves in my life.

Though I had my own financial and career goals in my life, I was equally inclined to get married and have babies after I got a good job.

To my heart's content, I got a job in my hometown, amused myself with the joy of gifting my grandmother. Parents and brother with my very first salary. I always had the proclivity for spreading joy & reciprocating the love & care in double.

Slowly evolving from a male bastion society, my generation allowed women to do higher studies and work before marriage. Nevertheless, in my period, it was still considered to be a late marriage. Then comes the call for marriage with no more time limit that I can avail, though it's an arranged marriage, my parents didn't ever instilled their views on me, they wanted me to put on the thinking cap, as I choose the groom among the choices they provide. Finally got alienated to one more lovely, charming and friendly relationship for life. Yes, I got married as it's a bare minimum dream right from childhood to be parents, cook your dishes, have your own house and remain happily ever after. That would be our favourite pretend and play in our childhood. I was never allowed to delude myself, as I strongly believed that I was going to have whatever wish for.

We were a happy couple with great understanding and also thought alike to have a baby as soon as possible, because we didn't believe spending time together as a couple for some time and then plan the baby later. As per our wish, we got pregnant in 3rd month of marriage and teared up in happiness. I was in Abu Dhabi when I knew this, we decided to fly back to India as his job demands him to be far away from me for most of the days. On reaching my in-laws' place, I could see a lot rejoiceful faces, celebrating the happiness more than I. Everything was going well until the 10th week of pregnancy. Until the doctor declared to do a medical abortion as they didn't find the baby's heartbeat even after enough wait period, though it's expected to see the heartbeat @ 6 weeks, she told the wait time uphill 10 weeks, so I stood positive that everything would be ok eventually. But unfortunately, it didn't. I did a medical abortion, though it was painful both emotionally and mentally, I overcame with a lot of confidence and endurance.

Exactly 6 Months after I got pregnant for the second time, this time along with happiness, came a lot of responsibility to stay happy and healthy, strictly to have a healthy baby. I was consciously cutting off slack on my every scan appointment. Music helped the greatest to wave down the anxiety I had.

On my 6th week scan, I witnessed the magic of being able to hear my baby's heartbeat for the first time. It felt like music to my soul and reassurance of a safe pregnancy ahead. My & baby was healthy and happy, outperformed all the scans, I felt so connected with the baby that I never felt lonely, though we are alone in flats, in Cochin. In the late second trimester, every kick of the baby reassured life and kept me excited to meet the little person very soon.

We were deliberately following a good diet, taking medicines regularly and were on time for all our scans. We are getting ready for one such scan day, after the usual ritual of prayer and wholesome breakfast, we headed towards the hospital. On our way to the hospital, I felt unusual cramping pain for a second, and it vanished, though it was a little haunting. My husband convinced me to tell anyway, we are going to meet the doctor, so nothing will happen. We proceeded to scan and had a thorough check up and felt relieved when I happened to hear the radiographer say that the baby is all healthy, and made me watch the baby's face, hands and legs. It was so therapeutic as those days scanning was my favourite part in hospital visit as I could have a glance of my baby, we were directed to the doctor's room to meet her, looking on to scan report and my progress in weight gain, the doctor waved a green signal towards great pregnancy ahead. Right before, we were exiting the room, my husband's memory transported to a previous visit where he recollects the doctor telling us that we have to take a transvaginal scan on our next visit, and he quickly reminded her about it too. Then the doctor took me to take a TV scan, we didn't know it was different from the normal scan.

We took a scan, she reconfirmed the baby's heartbeat and good growth with a smile, then she was astounded for a moment and told us to get admitted as I have to deliver in some time. I was stupefied, I didn't ask any questions; I simply sat in the wheelchair and was taken to the delivery room.

After reaching the room, I was informed that I had to deliver the baby as my cervix had opened completely, I didn't know what she talking about and was not interested to know it knowing either. All I wanted to know & ask the doctor was "is there any retort", but she told them they could have sutured even if they get a millimetre gap if noticed earlier. I was ticked off with her reply. If only she had mentioned the seriousness to me in our previous appointment, I would have been extra careful or found the best retort ourselves; all she asked us to do was remind her on the next scan. I was quizzing the nurse on how I would deliver a healthy baby. Will the baby survive? Is there anything that I can do to save the baby? They didn't answer any of my questions, rather gave me an injection to induce labour as labour didn't progress as such. Maybe my baby doesn't want to leave me, too. Despite the injection, my labour didn't proceed, I could feel the contraction, I was screaming in pain, I could feel something unusual happening inside my stomach, though I could also still feel the kicks of the baby then and there. As time progressed, I could see only darkness at the end of the tunnel.

My doctor left the place as her duty time got over, handing over to the nurse. I felt worthless, helpless and useless there. The nurse instructed me to push out to deliver the baby. Though I was screaming in pain, though I wanted to end the torture I am going through mentally and physically, I couldn't push because I was already informed that the baby can't survive if delivered as it's too early, even to get ventilation support. I felt like murdering a life inside me, I hated my body, I hated myself, I tried to hold the baby as possible as I could, though there is no hope. It's my way of cuddling, holding and caressing the baby one last time. And yeah, I am human, not superhuman. I couldn't handle the pain anymore and had to deliver the baby. I could hear nurses discussing that the baby is a girl and she is no more.

They took her away somewhere, showed her to my parents and brought her back to me to show her to me, for the first & last time.

But when they brought it next to me, I closed my eyes. I couldn't see her.

It took time for me to realise my body and mind, by the time I got ok physically, I started to investigate it and realised I lost my baby due to medical negligence. If she had noticed it earlier and done the needful, she could have been alive. It took a lot of time to get back to normalcy, it wasn't easy, it's not easy to excuse yourself or your own body like you excuse the doctor, even after the hate. I was guilty, depressed and heartbroken.

My husband helped me a lot to get me out of this, though even he was devastated. I was pregnant again, this time with the strongest support of husband, my parents, my brother, my periamma who were literally at my call as I advised bedrest throughout pregnancy with cervical cerclage, also relatives and friends who made sure of my wellbeing and did all little things to make me happy, last but not the least my grandmother and mothers influence in my life helped me a lot to stand against all the odds and be a parent at last as I wished for amidst all the situation. Both of them were so mentally strong, consistent, dedicated and grounded. I acquired all this not only because they preached to me to do so, but they have also been a living example. I am so lucky to have such inspiring and beautiful hearts around me. Of course, there were lots of ups and downs in my first delivery; end of the day, I had a beautiful baby boy who conquered my world. Followed by a second delivery in 2 Years, this time I prayed for a girl and was blessed with one. Though I had to face lots of struggles pre- and post-pregnancy, post both the deliveries, in a few years, everything fell in place, and we are happy now. All I did was stand strong with trust, and I always believed, after every storm it rains, and when it rains, it pours!

After all, Life is Plus, Minus and Equal.

Though I enjoyed motherhood with two beautiful kids. I always had the regret for not having a glance at her face. How would I correct this? How would I make her happy in heaven, ensure her she is most beloved, and she will be remembered forever? Life is very beautiful, we don't need to go out in search of answers for all your questions, it's very easy to get it accurately when searched inside you or get reference from your own life experience, The worthful solution I figured out is to offer a helping hand to children orphanage and fulfil their basic needs in every possible way I could especially on that specific day of the year. I am sure that sparkle in their eyes & smile on their lips makes her happy, and that gives me lots of strength and motivation to do more back to society.

PROUDLY AN ALCOHOLIC'S DAUGHTER

SRINITHI VARSHINI P

We all have our lowest of lows and highest of highs. We all are social animals, and we in some way or the other way seek some sort of validation from the people around us. For a few, it's friends and family; for some, it's society, and there are the rest who don't seek validation but are shaped like a diamond by filtering and constructively using the constant narratives of the world. This is the story of a girl who belongs to the latter - neither dependent nor independent, but interdependent.

Where do I want to start? One of the vivid memories of my childhood is the five-year-old me standing on my toes trying to peek through the hall window to see whether my dad was back home. I guess I was the only one who was happy about my dad's return after a long day at work. I never understood why everyone wasn't excited like I was. My dad was the kindest person I have ever met in my life. He gave as if he had the whole world's treasure with him when my mom was facing all the debts that we were immersed in. Sometimes, as an adult, I do wish I had remained a kid so that I wouldn't have treated him as all the other grown-ups saw him. I never thought I would become one of them. Okay!! I can understand that you are puzzled. My dad was an alcoholic. Though society had so many complaints about him, even I do, but apart from the addiction part, he is a good soul. If you are thinking it's either a sorrow story or going from rags to riches overnight. Oopsie! It's not.

To be honest, even though we have gone in search of my dad in the streets and carried him back home covered with mud and dirt, his bag always had a bottle of liquor along with what I asked for from the stationery for my project, to the savouries that I longed for. One part of the world never saw my father's good side, and those who did exploited his good side. It wasn't just him, but we all were in it together. There we were living a perfectly imperfect, flawed but beautiful father-daughter story amidst all the chaos. I felt it was unfair for the world to label me for something that I hadn't done wrong. Then one day I decided that if the world was going to define me by my father's weakness, then I am going to be proud of it because I am here despite all the imperfections. I guess it's not a common thing for a third grader to hear a thud while playing with her friends, just to realise her father had fallen without being able to walk properly and rush to him and carry him home. I have opened doors to my friends knocking just to say that your

dad is downstairs. Can you bring him home, coz we all are scared? To be honest, that very moment anger rushed to my head, but the second I saw my dad completely covered with dirt and smiling at me, all I remember feeling was that my dad was back home with me. I felt he was safe with me. I mostly sighed a relief. I have seen things more than a kid could understand. Despite hearing a lot of swear words, I have never once tried to use one. The shortcomings started fueling me.

In a world with so many parenting classes and books and with so much information just at our fingertips because of technology, I get awestruck by how my mom did all this by herself with no access to any of the above. She often says I never brought you up instead, I just tried to provide the right amount of water, sunshine, and soil for you to grow by yourself, though I couldn't provide all of that all the time. She always said that you are a wildflower. I hope that you all had A great childhood, but even the perfect family had imperfections, and we all might have felt like wildflowers sometimes. If you don't well I have felt that way. My mom lets us make our decisions after discussing with us the pros and cons of that. Learning something through experience isn't that easy. Sometimes my decisions had good outcomes, and sometimes I hit rock bottom both emotionally and physically. Either way, I am glad I had my family most of the time. The times they couldn't, I had my friends. Oh yeah! I got lucky there. Don't you think that sometimes we get so attached to people that we start making decisions for them? Sometimes in the name of love, we do live others' lives as well. No hard feelings, I accept that I have done that and realised a lot later that I was wrong. Looking back, I know that I was privileged enough to be an individual even as a kid and decide the course of my life. My mom kept it simple: you make a decision and you own its consequences. It was as simple as that for her. Because we all experienced and learnt different things from the different adventures that we went on, we all had different values, though we shared a few values as a family. With time, we learned to respect each other's values. I guess that's one important thing for any relationship to survive. Though our neighbours, colleagues, and family members had different opinions of our family, we got the best environment to learn and grow, though we all went through a rough patch. We were taken to book exhibitions and listened to debates, trying everything that I wished to, right from playing the Veena to playing Tennis. My mom was not just a drunkard's wife, but she was also a girl who dreamt of a life like all the others who claim to have a perfectly normal life. A woman with a lot of wisdom and potential to offer to the world, but wasted all of that so that she could at least try to give us a normal childhood. She was so brave and had a voice, but she feared one thing, a teeny tiny bit - society. She considered my father's habit might make people disrespect us and not treat us properly. Most of my friends and people linked to me and my brother never knew about it. Sometimes, because of that, I couldn't invite my friends to my home. During birthday parties, when my school friends asked about why my dad was blabbering or behaving like that, I didn't have an answer for it. I felt different. I felt as if I was someone I was not. I think this story might be a chance for me to open up and be who I am after all these years - a drunkard's daughter. No, I am in no way ashamed of it. I am so proud of it and how everyone tried their level best. As outsiders, we all judge others knowingly or unknowingly with all the things that we know and based on our experiences in life. Let alone my dad, I don't even know if I am perfect. My dad's imperfections were loud enough to be seen, but we all have something that we struggle with, which no one might know. It might be drugs, might be temptation, overeating, gossiping, attachment, etc. Who are we to judge and to be judged? I guess it's time for all of us with all areas of development to join hands to let people be who they are without the fear of being judged. To be honest, my mom fears that no one will accept me in their family as their daughter-in-law or wife for being a drunkard's daughter - if someone does that, it's purely their loss, and I for sure will smile at their ignorance. With my dad, we all learned a lot. Even my dad tried a lot to come out of his addiction. It wasn't a straight road for all of us in my family. Trust me, the lessons learned throughout this journey are so priceless. If I am given a chance once again, I will choose to be their daughter, though I would have done things a little differently by being kind to my mom and dad. To all those grown-ups whose family wasn't perfect, your inner child deserves to hear it this moment - don't be ashamed of the imperfections you were out of control. Be proud that you all made it despite all that, into the human being you are today. One thing that I learned as a kid was that I could either let the traumatic past ruin my future or be resilient and use the pain as a force for a better future. Now it's your turn to stream all those stories that control you to something that can empower you. Don't let whatever you went through trash. Your past has the potential for you to be the highest version of yourself.

THE MYSTERY WEDDING

RINI CATHERINE

It was a pleasant sunny morning in January 2014. The grand hall shimmered with flowers and lights, the stage adorned with maroon and white petals, creating an enchanting ambience. The flower man arrived with garlands, gleaming with gold and white flowers.

“Hey, how many people can the dining hall accommodate right now?” a voice echoed through the main hall. “The dining hall is almost empty, most guests have been served,” another voice replied from within.

Guests bustled in and out of the hall, each preparing for the event. New guests continued to arrive, filling the hall with smiles and excitement.

This was no ordinary occasion. It was Cathy’s wedding day!

The groom exuded confidence and sophistication as he stood tall in his navy-blue suit, the colour complementing his strong features. His patterned red tie added a bold yet refined touch to his ensemble, reflecting his vibrant personality. Every detail, from the crisp lines of his attire to the subtle gleam of his cufflinks, spoke of his impeccable taste and attention to style. As the cameras clicked away, capturing his every smile and gesture, it was evident that he was not only ready for his moment but also relishing every bit of it with grace and charm.

Meanwhile, Cathy lay in her bed, hardly aware of the festivities. Her hands were swollen from multiple IV needle insertions. Her family physician and a neurologist stood by her side, with a nurse assisting in her care. The room, which should have been adorned with jewels and silk, resembled a hospital ICU, filled with needles, medicines, and emergency kits. Cathy's family was anxious, unsure if she would wake up in time for the wedding.

At 7:15 am, a knock on the bride's room door interrupted the sombre scene. It was the groom's father, announcing that everyone was ready, and the bishop was on his way to the church. The wedding ceremony was scheduled for 7:30 am. However, Cathy remained in her nightdress, her veins filled with medication, and she was not fully conscious. Her parents could not help but wonder how different the day would have been if she had not been in that accident.

The day that changed everything

Two days before her wedding, Cathy returned from a church ritual, her home bustling with guests and laughter. It dawned on her that, despite being engaged for five months, she had not yet found a gift for her fiancé. She invited him to go shopping with her, and that evening, they embarked on their first pre-wedding date.

They visited a watch shop, where they found a pair of beautiful Titan watches. Cathy gifted one to her fiancé, and after a few more purchases, they rode back home on their bike. However, tragedy struck as they neared their house—Cathy fell from the bike, hitting the back of her head and lying unconscious on the road.

Her fiancé, shocked by the sudden turn of events, quickly called Cathy's parents, who rushed her to their family doctor. The accident would change everything.

The shocking report

After examining Cathy, the doctor recommended a CT scan as she remained unconscious. Cathy's family and her fiancé rushed her to the scan centre, and once the scan was completed, they admitted her to the local hospital for initial treatment until the report arrived.

The scan revealed a clot at the back of her head, requiring intensive care in the ICU. Meanwhile, at both the bride's and groom's homes, the relatives remained unaware of these developments, engrossed in the wedding preparations and attending to guests.

As the night wore on, some guests began to inquire about the bride and her parents. Rumours started to spread, shocking many and leaving others curious about the fate of the wedding. The news of Cathy's condition cast a shadow over the joyous occasion, with many expressing sympathies for the bride.

The doctor's advice

Amidst the wedding preparations, Cathy's condition took a dire turn as she began vomiting blood, alarming both her family and the attending doctor. Concerned, the doctor explained, "She's severely traumatised and requires intensive care in the ICU. If that's the case, we may need to cancel the wedding."

Cathy's family was devastated. Little did they anticipate that this joyous occasion would be turned on its head by such a predicament. They had invited 1500 guests, and a hundred close relatives were already gathered for the wedding. However, they were fortunate to have a skilled neurologist as a family friend and well-wisher.

The turn of events cast a sombre cloud over the once joyful occasion, leaving the family grappling with difficult decisions amidst their deep concern for Cathy's well-being.

The brave move

Cathy's family was renowned for their unwavering faith and resilience in the face of adversity. They had weathered many storms together, each time emerging stronger, their faith in their God unshaken. So, when tragedy struck on the eve of Cathy's wedding, they did not waver.

Despite the grim prognosis, Cathy's family chose to forge ahead, determined to make her dream wedding a reality. With the unwavering support of their family doctor and neurologist, they embarked on a journey of hope and determination. They transformed their home into a makeshift hospital, ensuring Cathy received the best care possible while simultaneously making arrangements for the wedding.

As the day of the wedding dawned, the family was faced with the daunting task of transporting Cathy to the wedding hall, located 25 kilometres away. It was tradition for the bride to arrive at the wedding hall before the groom, yet Cathy lay unconscious. With the aid of her mother and aunties, they carefully transported Cathy to the bathroom to prepare her. As the warm water cascaded over her, Cathy began to shiver violently, despite the comforting temperature. She trembled and tears streamed down her face, caught between pain and discomfort. Their resolve wavered momentarily as they realised the severity of her condition, fearing they might be endangering her life. Dread gripped them all as they grappled with the situation at hand. With sheer grit and determination, they managed to get her ready, although she was in excruciating pain and barely conscious.

Meanwhile, the groom and his family were preparing for the joyous occasion at their home. It sounds like Cathy's condition may have been a sensitive issue, but despite this, the hosts made a conscious effort to ensure that their guests didn't feel uncertain or uneasy about the wedding proceeding as planned. This demonstrates a level of grace and consideration on their part, acknowledging the importance of the occasion while handling a potentially difficult situation with care. Meanwhile, the photographers captured every moment, from the blessings of the family to the excitement of the groom as he set off for the wedding hall.

Back at Cathy's home, the photographers arrived, ready to capture the joyous moments of the bride getting ready. However, they soon realised that the atmosphere was sombre and tense. The doctors had strictly advised against using flash photography, as it could worsen Cathy's condition. Despite the challenges, the photographers managed to capture a few poignant images of Cathy, her face contorted in pain yet reflecting a quiet strength and determination.

The wedding ceremony at the church near the wedding hall was a bittersweet affair, filled with prayers and hopes for Cathy's recovery. It was a testament to the power of faith, love, and courage in the face of adversity. Despite the uncertainty and fear, Cathy and her family chose to celebrate life and love, inspiring all who witnessed their journey.

The reception night

The big day was nearly here—the wedding reception, the evening before the wedding. The hall shimmered with lights, creating a festive atmosphere. Everywhere you looked, there was a sense of joy and celebration. The wedding stage was adorned with green and white flowers, perfectly complementing the bride and groom's attire for the night.

The groom looked dashing in his sherwani, while Cathy was stunning in her light green silk saree. Together, they made a beautiful couple. Despite the challenges, Cathy had managed to get ready for the occasion with the help of various medications.

The betrothal ceremony was attended by 1500 guests, all gathered to celebrate the union of the couple. As a token of his love, the groom presented Cathy with a beautiful necklace. As he placed it around her neck, the guests couldn't help but exclaim, "Look, the groom is putting a necklace on the bride!" In their community, it was rare for the groom to gift jewellery, making Cathy's moment even more special. It was customary for only the groom's mother to adorn the bride with jewellery, and it was unheard of for the groom to gift anything other than the wedding ring. The guests marvelled at Cathy's luck! Indeed, Cathy was fortunate, not because her groom gifted her a necklace, but because, despite the unfortunate circumstances, he never wavered in his determination to marry her, no matter what!

Shortly after the betrothal ceremony concluded, Cathy found herself unable to stand on the stage any longer as the effects of the medication began to wear off, causing her pain to return. She was unable to join her groom in receiving guests on stage or in taking pictures with them. Disheartened, she retreated to her room.

From her window, Cathy watched as her groom stood alone on stage, receiving gifts from the guests. She felt a pang of sadness, realising that instead of a joyful occasion filled with love and laughter, they were missing out on creating beautiful memories together on stage.

Back to the wedding morning

After the doctors had administered the last of Cathy's medications, she was barely conscious. Despite this, her mother and cousins gently pulled her out of bed and prepared her for the wedding. Cathy wore no makeup, and her hair was simply combed and tied back with a loose rubber band. They avoided using any strong-smelling flowers or perfumes due to her condition. Instead, they adorned her with a weightless crown embellished with white stones and attached a white veil to it. Although she lacked the typical bridal accessories, she was still the epitome of beauty in the eyes of her groom.

From her childhood, Cathy had shared a special bond with her grandfather, who had passed away a few years before her wedding. As a poignant symbol of his presence, her family drove her to the church in her grandfather's red Chevrolet. It was as if her grandfather was accompanying her on this significant journey.

The wedding ceremony

As Cathy and her groom, Christopher, walked into the church, all eyes turned towards them. Many had doubted whether Cathy would make it to the wedding, but to everyone's surprise, she had managed to reach the church, a testament to her determination and the support of her family.

Despite being physically present in the church, Cathy was far from enjoying the events unfolding around her. The effects of the medication and the continuous pain in her head made it difficult for her to fully engage in the Holy Mass. She was drowsy and found it challenging to pray.

Finally, the moment arrived for the couple to exchange their wedding vows. The priest solemnly declared, "Since you intend to enter the covenant of Holy Matrimony, join your right hands, and declare your consent before God and his Church." Christopher spoke his vows before the Lord and the congregation, pledging his love and commitment to Cathy.

Then it was Cathy's turn. Despite her physical discomfort, she gathered all her strength and spoke her vows, "I, Cathy, take you, Christopher, for my lawful husband, to have and to hold from this day forward, for better, for worse, for richer, for poorer, in sickness and in health, until death do us part. I will love and honour you all the days of my life."

The priest blessed their rings, symbolising the eternal nature of their commitment, and asked the couple to exchange them. Christopher placed the ring on Cathy's finger, saying, "Cathy, receive this ring as a sign of my love and fidelity. In the name of the Father, and the Son, and the Holy Spirit." Cathy then did the same, exchanging rings with Christopher.

To symbolise their unity, the couple exchanged garlands, a traditional gesture of love and respect. Despite the challenges and adversity, Cathy and Christopher's love and commitment shone brightly, inspiring all who witnessed their union.

A deep sigh of relief

As soon as Cathy received her wedding ring, a profound sense of relief washed over not just her family but also Cathy herself. The unbearable pain seemed to vanish, and she became more aware of her surroundings. Her parents noticed that she appeared refreshed after the exchange of rings. What could have caused this sudden change?

Perhaps it was the Holy Sacrament of Marriage that refreshed her spirit. Or maybe she felt safe and secure in the love of her husband. It's also possible that she was relieved to have finally made it to the wedding, overcoming all the odds. Some even speculated that something miraculous had occurred during the ceremony. Whatever the reason, only God knows the true cause of this remarkable transformation.

After the ceremony concluded, the newlywed couple was driven back to the wedding hall in the same red Chevrolet.

They entered the hall hand in hand, walking up to the stage together. There, they welcomed a few important guests before Cathy began to feel the need to rest once more. She left her husband alone on stage and retired to her room, lying down on the bed.

As the last of the guests departed, Christopher walked into her room and sat by her side. Although she was unable to speak, Cathy could strongly feel his love for her, a silent reassurance of their bond in the face of adversity.

Happily, ever after

This couple has not only experienced true love on their wedding day but every day since then. Celebrating ten years of marriage, they have been blessed with two beautiful children, a boy, and a girl. Despite their imperfections, they firmly believe that together, they form a perfect couple and a perfect family. Their journey is a testament to the enduring power of love, showing that with dedication and faith, any challenge can be overcome.

ZOMBIE TO ZEN

NAVNEETHA

I, Navneetha, declare that whatever I share with you here is not a fiction. Ha ha..

I think I was studying in the 10th grade at that time. I studied in a government school in a small town in Tamil Nadu called Tiruchengode. Every class would have 40-45 students, and one teacher handles two subjects for four classes. You can imagine the load of exam papers a teacher has to correct after the exams. To tackle, some teachers hand-pick a few students from each class and ask them to correct 1-mark and 2-mark questions. Then the teacher corrects the 5-mark questions and 10-mark questions. Then she will give the papers to the students to total.

One day, our science teacher invited 7 of us from our class to her house for paper correction. I always like to host people. So, when we found out we were going to our teacher's house, I told my friends they could gather at my house and go to my teacher's house. And they all agreed. I was so happy to have my friends at my home. Then we all went to our teacher's house. We did the job we were supposed to do, along with having fun. It was already evening when we finished our work. It was time to leave. I think I got greedy. While leaving the teacher's house, I invited all my friends home. Everyone had a long day and was exhausted. So they all said they want to go to their home. But I was so adamant that they had to come to my home (what a childish behaviour!!) and when they said no, I got angry with all of them. I said furiously, 'ok, if you are not coming, fine. I am going home, and I moved my cycle without even looking at my friends and waving them bye. I returned home and was just refreshing. To my surprise, my friends stopped by my house before they left for their homes. They were so kind, they again came just because they didn't want to upset me.

Why am I talking about this incident? I was a real firecracker when I was younger, and that didn't change for quite a long time.

Many times, I have been reactive. When I think someone is being dishonest, someone is blaming me while I have done all the right things, someone is not doing their work, or when I know I am right and I have all the valid points to argue, I would react impulsively.

I always had the impression—this self-image—that I was short-tempered but honest. Whenever I got angry,

I believed it was for the right reasons. I didn't get upset easily or without cause; my anger always felt justified.

What wasn't fine, though, was how I expressed that anger.

Whenever I got angry, I ended up shouting at the other person. It wasn't deliberate — I didn't raise my voice consciously — but somehow, my tone would naturally become loud and sharp when upset.

This behaviour didn't stop even after I started working in an MNC. I remember once I scheduled a one-on-one with my manager. While he had processed US visas for two other teammates who joined with me, he had not processed one for me. This infuriated me. I started the conversation casually. As the conversation went on, my voice grew louder, too. My manager didn't say anything about that, and started the visa application process as soon as he returned to his desk after our meeting. Yet, later, I felt I didn't communicate in the correct way. What makes me say so? Because I didn't feel good after the meeting. I didn't feel great about my behaviour. Although in most instances, the situation turned in my favour, I realised this behaviour did not help me or others. I perceived it as an insult to others, and this bothered me deeply.

Fast forward a decade, now if you see me, I am all zen(!!!) most of the time? (!!!).. Even if that's not the case, I have figured out some important things about me, my mind and human psychology(ok, I am not a psychologist, but I guess life teaches us lessons where everyone can become a psychologist at one point). I think sharing those will be helpful to someone else who finds it challenging to change their behaviour.

Life happened. And family too! I had taken a sabbatical, and that's when it all started.

My son would leave the house at 7:40 a.m. for school, and my husband would leave at 8:30 a.m. for the office. From then on until 2:30 p.m., I had all the time in the world. My mind was completely free from all the work and financial commitments. It was under no stress. It was in no hurry. I was completely fulfilled, and this allowed the space to chew on my short temper and high tone when I got angry. This reflection time allowed me to observe my thoughts and feelings. I also had enough time to read as many books as I wanted. One of the subjects that I plunged into was emotions and managing them. My God, that was a complete revelation to me. I had never read any other self-help books except The Alchemist till then. So, when I started reading about emotions, it further fuelled my introspection. I started applying whatever I read and improved my EQ. I was in full research mode, and the research object was me.

Slowly, I became aware of how my body gives cues before I start shouting. Note that, at this point, I still have not avoided getting angry. I only became aware of my body's cues. I realised my heart was pounding faster as I entered an argument. After that pounding faster, I lost control of myself, and my voice went to its high.

Once I realised this, I started noticing whenever my heart pounded faster while arguing. As I shifted my focus to my body, I lost the urge to focus on the argument. This made me slow down. As I slowed down, my mind got enough time to think about the argument and gather enough information to communicate. Also, the slowdown time calmed me. Isn't this magical?!!! (Technically, if you lose control over yourself when you are emotional, it is called Amygdala Hijack! Our premature brain takes over the rational brain, and we do all the 'unwise' things and regret them later when we regain control.)

Slowly, very slowly, but steadily, I started gaining control over raising my voice. It gave me a sense of peace, satisfaction, and happiness that I am working on myself. What made me happiest was that we can change ourselves whenever we want.

My personal development journey in managing my anger continued. The next thing I did was to figure out the situations that made me angry. (Technically, these are called 'triggers' or 'push buttons.' You get angry or triggered when someone touches those 'push buttons.)

Figuring out these situations helped me prepare for similar moments in the future. I became aware that I got angry when my children didn't listen to me or made me repeat myself. I also got angry when someone didn't do their job correctly. Little by little, I started to recognise these patterns. Of course, I didn't sit down and write a list — but my mind began to notice and mentally keep track of these situations.

So, the next time my children didn't listen to me immediately, instead of getting angry, I paused. I didn't want to shout at them for two reasons. One, literally, after every 'getting angry and shouting' episode, I was physically and mentally tired. Next, I realised I was becoming a bad role model for children. I was teaching them that they can shout when they get angry. This very thought terrified me. So, these made me think, what can I do when they don't listen to me? So, I paused. I kept my voice normal, but my tone firm. I told firmly, 'Can you do this? I feel tired if I repeat.' This worked. They listened to me when I shared my thoughts and feelings like this. (Technically, as a Communication Coach, I tell my clients this. Tell the other person your feelings and needs instead of ordering them, shouting at them or blaming them.)

Similarly, I started thinking about how to reframe my sentences for the other situations. I badly wanted my peace all the time, which motivated me to constantly try correcting my responses.

This stage is done. In the meantime, I also worked on Communication techniques that I could use in these difficult situations.

I moved to the next stage. That is, diving into the reasoning of why something made me angry. (Technically, why should there be 'push buttons' or 'triggers' at all in the first place?) This opened a new Pandora's box, which I will not investigate in detail, as I know I could have already exhausted you. When I started analysing why something made me angry, it all boiled down to me. My mindset, my expectations, my attitude, my perspectives and I realised it had nothing to do with the other person. Literally!! It is not that I am a bad person or that I had a bad attitude. This is a truth that applies to each one of us. When you get angry, it is not the other person's fault. It is a fact that one of your expectations or needs is unmet. That's it. Most of the time, we think that the other person is the reason why we got angry. But I realised that's not the case.

I took ownership of my behaviour and feelings when I realised this, which changed everything. I don't hold any grudges towards the other person or their behaviour.

Now I have reached a phase. Whenever I know I am getting angry or something is bothering me, before yelling out, I think, "Why does this make me angry in the first place?" Most of the time, the answer to that question is that my expectations have not been met.

So, now that I know the unmet expectations behind my anger, I communicate those expectations instead of telling how the other person should behave. I may still have my push buttons, but that's okay. I now have the tools and experience to deal with those when they are pushed.

Isn't that zen?!

Had I had this knowledge in 10th grade, I would have thanked my friends for coming over in the morning and waved a happy goodbye when they wanted to go to their homes in the evening.

I would have still scheduled that one-on-one with my manager for visa, but I would have coolly stated what I wanted to say.

But that's fine. It‘s all in the game of life.

All this happened when I had time and my mind was stress-free. I slowed down in my work, and it helped me pace up my personal development. I am not telling anyone to give up their work for personal growth. But I firmly believe that taking up only what we can do and slowing down makes room to reflect on ourselves. I have become so passionate about this topic that you can contact me anytime to discuss this further.

I decided on the title for this story as soon as I got the theme. When I was writing this story, my friend from Canada called me one evening. She told me,' You know what? When I was messaging you, my daughter asked me who I was chatting with. I told her your name. And she told me, 'Oh, that's your 'zen' friend!!!'

Is that a coincidence planned by the Universe?

PREVIOUS BOOK BY DR. PRAVEEN SRINIVASAN

Available at

Amazon: https://amzn.in/d/9nGbXD4

Ziffybees: https://www.ziffybees.com/product/7-by-dr-praveen-srinivasan/

Book Trailer: https://youtu.be/bhkwv3hvVvw?si=hPYX-xSRuMLa2098

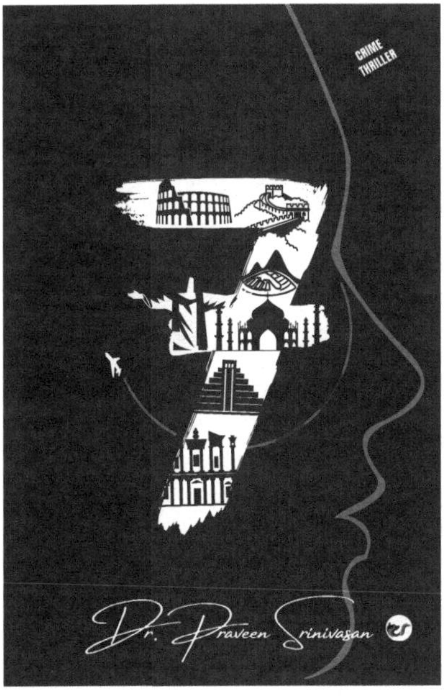